> Linda
> May the Lord continue to bless your life. Thank you so much for treating me as one of your own. You are a beautiful mother and have strong characteristics as a Proverbs 31 woman
>
> Paul

CROWNS DO BLOSSOM

A PROVERBS 31 WOMAN

S Paul Brooks

STEPHEN PAUL BROOKS

Copyright © 2015 by Stephen Paul Brooks

Crowns Do Blossom
A Proverbs 31 Woman
by Stephen Paul Brooks

Printed in the United States of America.

Edited by Xulon Press

ISBN 9781498438872

All rights reserved solely by the author. The author guarantees all contents are original and do not infringe upon the legal rights of any other person or work. No part of this book may be reproduced, stored in a retrieval system, or transmitted in any form or by any means without expressed written permission of the author. The views expressed in this book are not necessarily those of the publisher.

Unless otherwise indicated, Scripture quotations taken from The Complete Jewish Bible: An English Version of the Tanakh (Old Testament) and B´rit Hadashah (New Testament) by Jewish New Testament Publications, Inc. Clarksville Maryland USA, Jerusalem Israel. All rights reserved.

www.xulonpress.com

NAME	SYMBOL		NAME	SYMBOL
ALEPH	א		LAMED	ל
BET/VET	ב		MEM	מ ם
GIMEL	ג		NUN	נ ן
DALET	ד		SAMECH	ס
HE	ה		AYIN	ע
VAV	ו		PE/FE	פ ף
ZAYIN	ז		TZADI	צ ץ
CHET	ח		KOF	ק
TET	ט		RESH	ר
YUD	י		SIN/SHIN	ש
CHAF	כ ך		TAU	ת

ACKNOWLEDGMENTS

I want to thank my co-worker Jennifer Gross who sacrificially typed the original manuscript day in and day out for months. Your patience and having to retype numerous changes was much appreciated. May the Lord Jesus bless your faithfulness to this blessed project! I also want to thank my co-worker, Thad Aragon for working on my computer software and keeping it functioning, especially during the final weeks of typing. I also want to thank Rick Molina for helping me get a job working under a contract for Customs Border Patrol. This wonderful job gave me the finances and time to work this manuscript. Also, I would like to recognize my co-worker Juan Borrego for his excellent leadership skills and serving the President of the United States, as a Marine, under President George Walker Bush's term. Truly a job well done. To those who have had such an impact in my ministry I want to thank you for all the encouragement. Pastor Jack and Sharon Brock, Pastor Tim Brock, Pastor Perry and Amy Koehne and Christ Community Church in Alamogordo, New Mexico. I want to thank Ron and

Debbie Acton for their Christ-like leadership in the Body of Christ in El Paso, Texas. I want to recognize my good friend and brother in Jesus Christ James Isley. I want to thank Coronado Baptist Church in El Paso, Texas for their great leadership in and through the lives of many saints of the Lord Almighty. To my son Brandon Paul Brooks, brother Marc Brooks and son-in-law Jesse William Palacio, thank you for loving your families and working hard to give them a blessed life. To all my buddies who love me unconditionally, my grandsons; Brandon Paul Jr, Joseph, Ethan, Jacob, Chase, and Cameron. I want to give special thanks to the staff at Xulon press for assisting and helping to process this manuscript into a fine "tapestry of linen." May this book enrich your lives as it has my life in keeping God's Word true to our hearts.

In memory of my uncle, Le Grosdidier who wrote this poem to his beautiful wife aunt, Marie.

THE ROSE AND YOU

The beauty and essence
of the rose is splendor
I love to look at it
so fragile
so tender
All flowers are beautiful
but the rose stands out
To be the most perfect
almost without doubt
The fragrance sweet
sets it apart
It's pleasingly subtle
It appeals to your heart
As your natural beauty
with the rose I compare
Our love for each other
is pleasant to share
So I whisper to you
with feelings true
Come into the garden with me
I want my roses to see you

DEDICATION

I want to dedicate this book to some very special and loving women in my life. First, my wife Kimberly, "My Love." You have been and still are an amazing woman of the Lord Jesus Christ. Your faith in the Lord is inspirational to me and all of the family. This book was inspired by you and a gift well deserved. I truly love you. To my sister Dr. Lynn Brooks. From my heart I want to thank you for sacrificing your life and taking me into your home. Your courage and determination literally saved my life spiritually, emotionally, and physically. To my beautiful daughter Lynne Brooks Palacio, no father could ask for a better daughter. May this book bless your life as you live out its Truth. To my daughter-in-law Janette Guardado Brooks who works so hard as a business woman and raising four boys, I honor your strong spirit. I see strong qualities of a Proverbs 31 woman revealed in your character and life. Thank you for loving my grandsons the way you do. To my sister-in-law Ana Marie Schaeffer Brooks, I want to thank you for your most loving and kind heart. You are a true reflection of God's love and "hesed" which means over abundant kindness. You are the Naomi and Ruth in the lives you touch daily. To my nieces Faith Marie Brooks Nulk and Rose Michelle Brooks Everhard, I am joyful you are both women of faith in Jesus Christ. Thank you for loving me as you do. I am honored and proud to be an uncle of you both. May this book be a blessing and an encouragement as you both walk with the Lord Jesus in and through His Word. Last but not least, I dedicate this book to the one for whom all of the Brooks boys have been patiently waiting. Kimberly Brooke, the granddaughter we have all prayed and hoped would grace our family one day. Your arrival in June 2015 will not come soon enough. May this book, one day, reflect all that Gods wants you to be in Him.

HOLY INSPIRATIONAL SCRIPTURE

"Revelation 19:11-13- "Next I saw heaven opened, and there before me was a white horse. Sitting on it was the one called Faithful and True, and it is in righteousness that he passes judgment and goes to battle. He eyes were like a fiery flame, and on his head were many royal crowns. And he had a name written which no one knew but himself. He was wearing a robe that had been soaked in blood, and the name by which he is called is, THE WORD OF GOD.""

Psalm 137:5-6–"If I forget you, Yerushalayim, may my right hand wither away! May my tongue stick to the roof of my mouth if I fail to remember you, if I fail to count Yerushalayim the greatest of all my joys."

Genesis 12:1-3–"Now Adonai said to Avram, "Get yourself out of your country, away from your kinsmen and away from your father's house, and go to the land that I will show you. I will make of you a great nation, I will bless you, and I will make your name great; and you are to be a blessing. I will bless those who bless you, but I will curse anyone who curses you; and by you all the families of the earth will be blessed."

HATIKVAH "The Hope"

>As long as the Jewish spirit is
>yearning deep in the heart
>
>With eyes turned toward the East,
>looking toward Zion
>
>Then our hope-the two-thousand-
>year old hope will not be lost
>
>To be a free people in our land
>
>The land of Zion and Jerusalem

CONTENTS

PROLOGUE	....	xv
INTRODUCTION	....	xix
1	WHO CAN FIND?	 27
2	HER HUSBAND TRUSTS HER	 37
3	SHE WORKS	 49
4	SHE PROCURES	 59
5	SHE IS LIKE	 71
6	IT'S STILL DARK	 79
7	SHE CONSIDERS	 89
8	SHE GATHERS	 99
9	SHE SEE'S	 109
10	SHE PUTS	 119
11	SHE REACHES	 129
12	WHEN IT SNOWS	 139
13	SHE MAKES	 149
14	HER HUSBAND IS KNOWN	 159
15	SHE MAKES LINEN GARMENTS	 169
16	CLOTHED WITH STRENGTH	 179

17 WHEN SHE OPENS	189
18 SHE WATCHES	199
19 HER CHILDREN ARISE	209
20 MANY WOMEN	219
21 CHARM CAN LIE	229
22 GIVE HER A SHARE	241
23 CONCLUSION	251
24 ENDNOTES	253
BIBLIOGRAPHY	261

PROLOGUE

I can vividly recall the day in which the revelation of God was deposited into my spirit. It was in the evening. The sun had dissipated behind the Franklin Mountains in El Paso and the street lamps had come on. I was approximately seven years old at the time. My oldest sister Lynn and I were walking up the sidewalk on Lebanon Street, snacking on a bologna sandwich and potato chips. She began to talk to me about the Lord and how He was seated on a throne with angels all around Him. My thoughts of God in heaven become a spiritual reality. The realness of God became a truth in my spirit. I was aware that my two-dimensional world was gone. A spiritual existence enveloped me and I believe I became spiritually alive that night by the Holy Spirit.

As I look back on that wonderful revelation of the Creator, I realized I was embraced and loved by a female during my experience with the Lord Almighty. My sister loved me in her uniqueness, as a believer of Yeshua (Jesus). She introduced me to the Living Savior. I needed my sister's love. I trusted her and knew she loved me very much. We as brother and sister needed each other. We lived in a home of horrid abuse; a home of hate and violence.

Eventually, my sister reached the age of adulthood and got married. It was devastating to see her leave but life had to go on. Little did I realize, my Heavenly Father was moving my sister in a direction to gain the spiritual fortitude and financial ability to help me escape the abuse I had experienced. My "bondage in Egypt" was quickly coming to an end, as God was molding her into a true **Proverbs 31 women.**

Unfortunately my mom was unable to really care and nurture me the way my sister did. She was an abused wife who was fighting cancer. Her bones were brittle and she lived in tremendous pain. I was a thirteen year old teenager who learned to feed her and help her with basic daily needs. She always thanked me for being gentle and having patience as I assisted her in and out of the wheel chair and hospital bed at home. The love she showed me was lost in July of 1973. I was now at home with three other siblings struggling to survive each day hoping to not be mentally and physically abused by our dad.

The only people I could ever trust were females in my life. They were flowers in my life and a crown to my head. My sister was planning out an escape and she used a lawyer to lay the foundation of salvation from an abusive dad. When I was fifteen, we planned out an escape that literally took my dad by surprise. She took me and my siblings one evening when my dad was gone and led us to freedom for the first time in our lives. He came home to an empty house and a drafted letter by our lawyer. He never bothered or hurt us again. A female with strength and courage came to my rescue. If that was not enough of a blessing, my future (and beautiful) wife lived not far from my sister's home. She played a major role in my young life back then. God had a plan for us to meet and become husband and wife. The Lord blessed me with wonderful women who would encourage me and help me to achieve His highest and best for my life.

As life went on I built a career in aviation maintenance. But my heart has always been to study God's Word which eventually would lead me to Bible school at Southwestern Assemblies of God University. Years later I began a study in the original Hebrew language of the Scriptures. I memorized each Hebrew letter and learned to write them in block form. I wanted to study Hebrew and learn how to know God from the original script.

One day I noticed ***Proverb 31:10-31*** used Hebrew letters acrostically and I wanted to know the reason. Why is a female described with proverbs using each individual Hebrew Letter? What is God trying to say about an honored female in ***Proverbs 31***? This journey for me has answered the question as to why my sister came to my rescue. I have found my answer in these proverbs with each Hebrew letter. God can and does accomplish His miracles as much through women as He does men.

I want to close this prologue now without an end but rather as a continuous journey watching God use females in my life and ministry to help me continue obeying His will. Women are blooming crowns of gold that continue the legacy of ***Proverbs 31***.

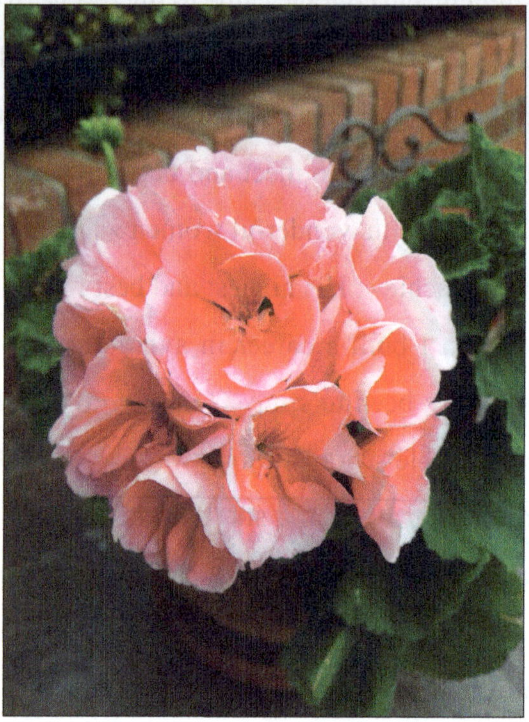

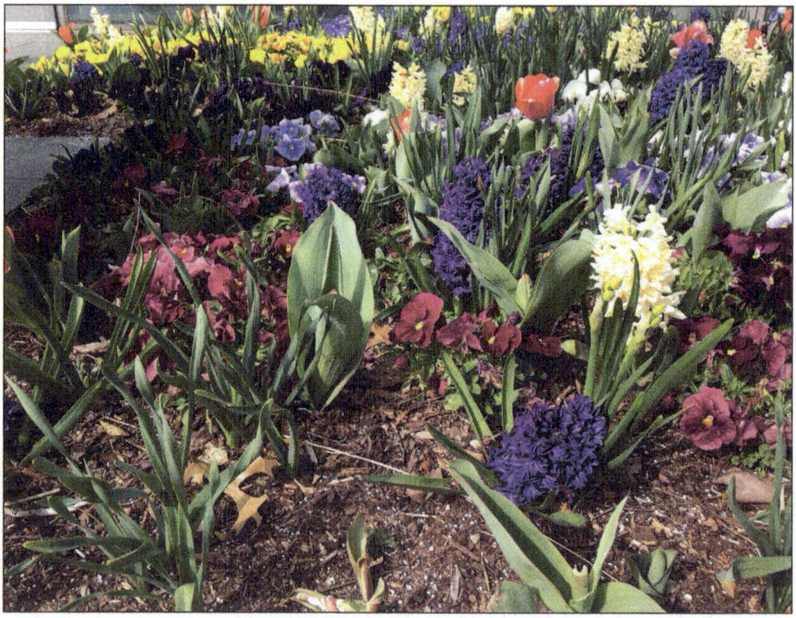

CROWNS DO BLOSSOM

INTRODUCTION

"Then God caused a deep sleep to fall upon the person; and while he was sleeping, he took one of his ribs and closed up the place from which he took it with flesh. The rib which Adonai, God, had taken from the person, he made a woman-person; and he brought her to the man person. The man-person said, "At last–! This is bone from my bones and flesh from my flesh. She is to be called Woman (Hebrew: ishah), because she was taken out of Man (Hebrew: ish)." (Genesis 2:21-23)

Adam became aware of his own exceptional status and solitariness by observing the complementary pairings of male and female among the other animate beings.[1] The Lord empathizes with Adam's loneliness, so instead of taking a dusty clay like red substance from the earth and breathings life into it, as He did Adam; the Father, Son, and Spirit create a women in a most unique fashion. God took the initiative to provide the wife for Adam.[2] She is going to be a suitable companion and she will become his equal and united with her husband as one.

In her creation story, God puts Adam in a deep sleep and takes a rib and some flesh from his side. Literally, the Lord "built,"[3] the women. "In a word play, Genesis Rabba 18:1 connects the present use "to build" with "to discern" indicating that the "women was endowed with intelligence surpassing that of man."[4] The Hebrew word "to build" has a very similar spelling as "to discern." This intelligence in a woman is at a higher spiritual level than the man.

This reality of an intelligent discerning woman is recognized weekly in a most unique and special fashion. Each week on the sixth day evening, preparation is made to celebrate the seventh day of the week called "Shabbat." The faithful Jewish community obeys Adonai and observes this day as a day to remember His creation. The home is cleaned and the dinner is prepared. The family bathes and dresses up in anticipation of the start of Shabbat.

As the sun sets and the sixth day comes to a close, the wife lights two candles and welcomes the start of Shabbat by prayer to Adonai. The family can go to a brief worship service at the local synagogue. Upon arriving home, the father blesses his children then sings a hymn of praise to his faithful wife from ***Proverbs 31:10-31***.

The husband is reciting in song and praise, a prophetess's prophecy that was spoken to a King of Israel. This prophecy reveals the wonders of a female and, I believe, gives later generations the opportunity to "listen, learn, and live more richly."[5]

The female, the crown of creation, is adored, loved, and highly respected among her husband and children. In the spiritually rich environment of honoring the Lord, a wife's complex design, that is wonderfully magnificent, is praised by the leadership of the home. Her character and the spiritual richness of the Torah in her heart blooms and brings the aromatic fragrance of God's eternal mysterious love among the family. On this weekly festive day, the wife and mother is honored by the delight of her husband and indirectly, the children, as he serenades his wife with his love using the words of this proverbial prophecy.

As a matter of scriptural fact, ***Proverbs 31*** reveals a contrast to the androcentric world of mankind. These twenty two proverbs about a noble wife reveals a female who is proactive outside the home as well as in the home. First, let me say these proverbs destroy the man-made system of male domination through the male dominated mindset. A women was never created to be subjected to the confines of a domesticated home. If you, a female, feel suppressed by a male dominated world, these proverbs will help you liberate yourself to be the woman Adonai the Lord, designed you to be, for His glory and honor.

This prophecy reveals a proper relationship of a wife to her husband and children. She is not a slave to the whims of a man or to the children. It is an assault upon the Lord to misdirect His truth about the value and place of women. She is an ambassador and representation of God's care and love to the whole world rather than becoming a servant slave under a man-made philosophy.

Before we can really get to the heart of each proverb, it is important to grasp a little history in the creation of the Bible. Originally the ancient text was written in Hebrew. Paleo-Hebrew namely. Each Hebrew letter "represented both a sound and a picture."[6] The twenty two letters tell a story of Yeshua's (Jesus') love and the Good News of His salvation. When Moses scripted the Torah on Mount Sinai he wrote in pictographic Hebrew. Even King David wrote in the ancient Semitic characters. Eventually the letters changed into a more squared off form,[7] possibly during the time of Ezra and Nehemiah. But the Torah scholars never forgot the original meaning of each Hebrew letter and some today still write in the ancient script.

Why this brief history lesson on the ancient pictographic script? Due to the fact that each Hebrew letter has a particular meaning about God and His created world, besides the sounds that convey His truth in conceptual form, it impacts the interpretation of ***Proverbs 31:10-31*** and how we will approach it exegetically. We will see the literal interpretation and the hinting interpretation as well.

Each proverb starting with ***Proverbs 31:10***, is assigned or starts with a Hebrew letter alphabetically. There are twenty two proverbs in ***Proverbs 31:10*-31**, hence twenty two Hebrew letters acronymically. If you have a somewhat accurate translation of the Bible it will show,

Introduction

in Hebrew script form, a Hebrew letter in front of each particular proverb from verses 10-31.

Each Hebrew letter starting with "Aleph" and ending with "Tav" conveys a pictorial concept, along with its symbolic meaning, that highlights or better explains each proverb about a female. Each letter along with its companion proverb is a "midrash" or teaching about a unique characteristic of a women. She embodies eternal realities about Yeshua Messiah (Jesus the Messiah) letter by letter. In and through her, each pictographic letter with its symbolic spiritual meaning is revealed by her spiritual and physical activities.

Ultimately as you study **_Proverbs 31_**, it reveals Jesus Christ in a most unique manner. He has actually attached Himself letter by letter in this prophetic praise and teaching about a noble female. Let me explain. In the original Hebrew text of ***Isaiah 41:4*** the Lord calls himself "Aleph-Tav." This is the first and last letter of the Hebrew alphabet which means in translation, God is the first letter to the last letter of the Hebrew alphabet. ***Zechariah 12:10*** identifies, in Hebrew, the sacrificial Savior, Yeshua is a person called the "Aleph-Tav."[8] In ***Revelation 1:8*** Christ says,

> *"I am the 'A' and the 'Z,'" says Adonai, God of heaven's armies, the One who is, who was and who is coming" (Revelation 1:8).*

This translation back into Hebrew means He is the "Aleph-Tav." Yeshua (Jesus) identifies Himself as the whole of the pictographic Hebrew alphabet. He is the perfect representation of each Hebrew letter in its complete fullness. The noble female manifests these characteristics in her own unique created design as we read in *Genesis* and *Proverbs.*

Some scholars say that each Hebrew letter is used acrostically as an aid to memory retrieval as the husband sings to his wife on Shabbat. I agree, but that seems to be too simple an exposition. I believe God is hinting at a deeper and more spiritually rich revelation of Himself in and through a female. I think the Father, Son, and Holy Spirit can be seen in this beautiful creation that He gave to Adam and any other man who is blessed to have such a wife.

As we open up to *Proverbs 31:1*, we discover a King who is speaking a prophecy his mother verbally dictated to him. "It is a prophecy given by inspiration and direction of God," through a mother.[9] She is not happy with her son's behavior concerning women and his strong alcoholic drinking habits. Her son, the King, needs to live righteously before the Lord and be an advocate for the poor and needy.

This prophecy can be an instruction to daughters or a direction for men.[10] As you read *Crowns Do Blossom*, each chapter will describe each particular Hebrew letter pictographically and symbolically. Then each parable unique to their assigned letter, will be explained by its simple literal meaning and eventually into a deeper and richer exposition. You the reader will discover how a righteous woman can express each Hebrew letter in her practical as well as spiritual lifestyle. Her reactive movements to the family dynamics will be discovered and this is why a noble wife is honored by a song of praise each week during Shabbat.

I have given you several blank pages at the end of each chapter to write your thoughts and emotional answers to challenging questions about what you have read. I also encourage you, as a female, to select a biblical woman who best represents each proverb and even a contemporary female who has impacted your life spiritually. I did select a woman from Scriptures I felt best represented a particular Hebrew letter. I wrote about her in one of the chapters. She is hidden and you will find her.

I would like to honor my Savior Jesus Christ by using His Hebrew name, Yeshua, throughout the rest of this book. May the Father, Son, and Spirit be lifted up and glorified as you read this tribute to all the females both young and seasoned. May God bless all who read this book! My hope is that you will discover a richer and more rewarding experience with the Lord and your family. You, as a female, can be a crown that blossoms.

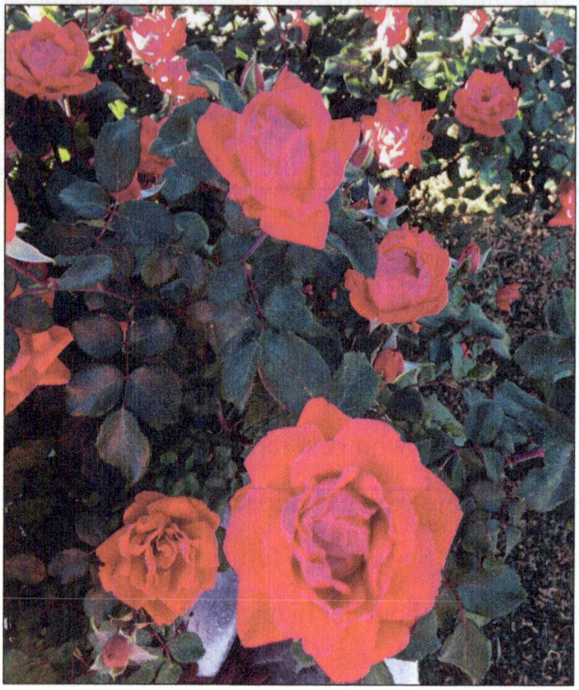

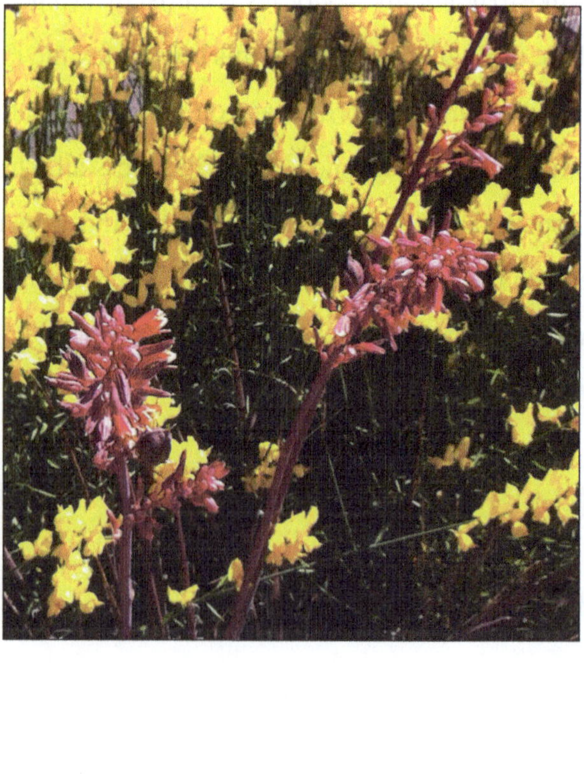

Chapter 1

WHO CAN FIND?

"Who can find a capable wife? Her value is far beyond that of pearls." (Proverbs 31:10)

"The first letter of the Hebrew alphabet is called "*Aleph*" (pronounced "ah-lef").[11] It is a silent letter but takes on the vowel sound associated with it. The Paleo-Hebrew shape depicts an ox or a bull.[12] The pictographic concept conveys strength, leader, the first, what or who will lead you, what is most important, or what gives strength.[13] The ox also represents a patient animal that serves mankind and it is used upon the altar as a sacrifice to God.[14]

Even though this is a silent letter its meaning is very powerful. Strength of leadership can be deafening in its silence. Strength of spirit and mind is not inclusive to men. A female who spends time with Yeshua Messiah will take on the leadership and strength of the Holy Spirit. It's the anointing of the Spirit that can bring a woman the godly characteristics of "Aleph." Walking and living in the Father's eternal strength is one has who grasped His Torah and understands who it speaks about, namely Yeshua Messiah. Deborah was such a woman who, through her spiritual strength from the Lord, caused Him to bless the land of Israel with peace and rest for forty years *(See* **Judges 4-5)**.

A well-known Hebrew word beginning with the letter "Aleph" is "'ab-ba" which means "dear Father."[15] He is One whom will lead you and is most important.

We read in **Galatians 4:6,** *"Now because you are sons, God has sent forth into our hearts the Spirit of His Son, the Spirit who cries out, "Abba!" (that is, "Dear Father!").*

Our Father is our strength and eternal leader. He is most important above all things whether it be spiritual, emotional or physical. We acknowledge Him as our source of strength and salvation and in Him and through Him we know He will lead us into all Truth.

Another Hebrew word is "e-ven pin-nah" which means cornerstone.[16] The first stone laid that will be a reference for all other stones to be positioned, as a structure is built, is called the chief cornerstone. The walls around the old city of Jerusalem were constructed by using cornerstones. Archeological research and digging has revealed these massive cornerstones and you can see them as you walk along the tunnels next to the Wailing Wall. It led the builders as they constructed this massive wall of strength and defense.

A last example of a Hebrew word using the letter "Aleph" is "'em" which means mother.[17] No surprise mother in Hebrew starts with the letter "Aleph". A child relies on the strength of the mother's

Who Can Find?

nourishment to sustain life. To a baby, the most important leader is their mother. Even in life's journey, a child usually will always go to the mother for sustained leadership and strength. Even during war as soldiers died on field, their last words were calling out for their mother. Their last sustaining drops of life giving blood and air in their lungs gave voice in honor of the strong one who nourished and loved them as a child. Her enduring patience and servant-hood to her children will teach and train them on how to love and be loved. She is a blessing of added strength to any man who is given God's grace in finding such a soulmate.

This proverb describes a man diligently searching by enquiring, discovering and laying hold of a virtuous female of noble character. The woman designed by God is of moral goodness and admirable among society. *(See Philippians 4:7-8.)* Her spiritual strength guides her as she understands her strength comes from the Lord. In the Lord, she holds a Christ-like excellence and is in service to the King of Kings, Yeshua the Messiah. Her strength reveals the passion and heart of Yeshua's characteristics.

> *"For this very reason, try your hardest to furnish your faith with goodness, goodness with knowledge, knowledge with self-control, self-control with perseverance, perseverance with godliness, godliness with brotherly affection, and brotherly affection with love. For if you have these qualities in abundance,*

they will keep you from being barren and unfruitful in the knowledge of our Lord, Yeshua, the Messiah."
(See 2Peter 1:5-8.)

This type of woman is a strong leader who can co-lead and guide the home. Her inward worth is of value to a husband and he recognizes she actively worships the Lord while she herself hopes she will be recognized as having equal worth to the husband by God's grace and love.

A husband is so blessed to have a wife such as this that her worth to him, exceeds his limited expectations. She, in his heart, is far past super-abounding in spiritual gifts and blessings from the Lord Almighty. She brings joy, wisdom and spiritual surplus to the marriage. Her intelligence and godly attitude reflect and ensure great fruitfulness to the home by a display of leadership and enduring strength.

<u>Her intelligence and godly attitude reflect and ensure great fruitfulness to the home by a display of leadership and enduring strength.</u>

Concerning her value, it is likened to pearls or precious stones. Figuratively, her value exceeds even the pearls used on the gates of the New Jerusalem *(Revelation 21:21)*. An honorable woman full of the Spirit *(Ephesians 5:18-20)* can be found by searching diligently. A female graced by God's blessing is of extreme value to her husband. Wealth and gaiety are favorable but to have such a capable wife exceeds the material and emotional blessings of the richest sort.

These qualities of a wife mirror the letter "Aleph". A noble intelligent wife gives strength to the home. She will help lead the home by her spiritual leadership. This is possible from a women who is blameless and lives under God's Torah. She seeks the Lord wholeheartedly and observes, with care, His instruction that says,

"How happy are those whose way of life is blameless, who live by the Torah of Adonai" (Psalms 119:1)!

Yeshua Messiah is the perfect image of "Aleph". He is the first of all things and His strength surpasses all greatness. A capable wife will seek her strength from the True Leader who is the perfect image of the Father. *(See Colossians 1:15-20.)* Her strong and momentous Savior displays perfect leadership and she can operate in God's strength and grace by His example. Her ability to co-lead the home comes from His eternal power, mercy, and grace.

"God has spoken once, I have heard it twice: strength belongs to God. Also to you Adonai, belongs grace; for you reward all as their deeds deserve" (Psalms 62:12(11)-13(12)).

Yeshua wills to bless the leadership of the marriage, which includes the virtuous wife, with the strength of the Spirit.

This outpouring of the Spirit will enable the wife of supreme worth to solidify her praise to God by living out His characteristics of strength and leadership. She will know by her spirit it is most important to bring these godly characteristics to the home. She is a competent, God-fearing, honest, and incorruptible woman of the Lord.

A godly wife with a strong spirit also simulates a judge. In *Exodus 18:13-23*, Moses' father-in-law respectfully requested the attention of Israel's leader when recommending the selection of judges among the Israelites who are God-fearing, honest and incorruptible. These traits can only come to fruition through a strong leader. A blessed man who can find such a wife with these qualities can build a home to the glory of God along with her strength and leadership.

> *"A capable wife is a crown for her husband, but a shameful one is like rot in his bones." (Proverbs 12:4)*

Let Us Reason Together

What is your concept of the *Proverbs 31* woman?

Who fits that description in your life?

What do you find easiest about living the *Proverbs 31* lifestyle?

What's most difficult for you?

What questions, thoughts or feelings do you have after reading chapter one?

NOTES

NOTES

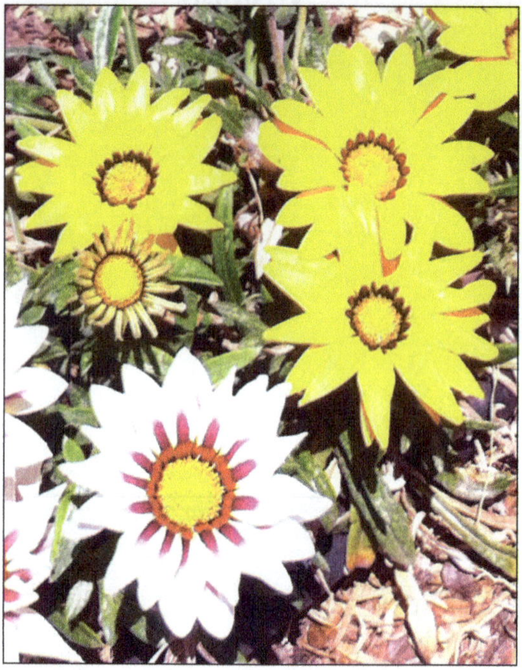

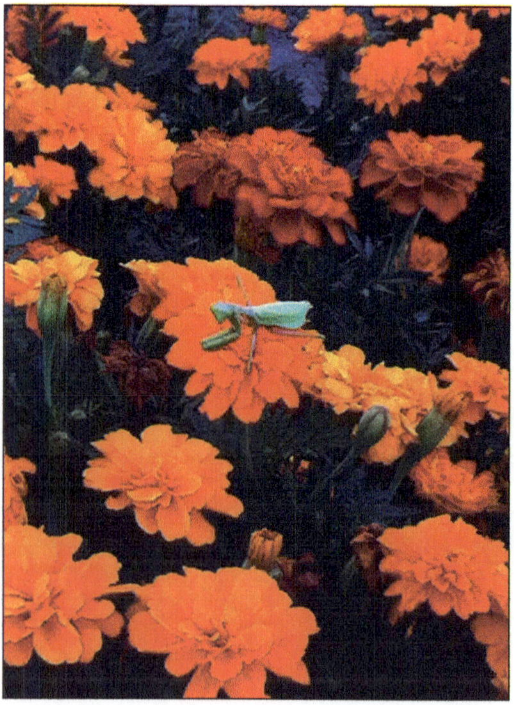

Chapter 2

HER HUSBAND TRUSTS HER

"Her husband trusts her from his heart, and she will prove a great asset to him." (Proverbs 31:11)

The second letter of the Hebrew alphabet is called "*Bet*" (pronounced "bait")[18] Its sound is "b" as in "bat." The pictographic shape is a tent, or wall of a house.[19] Symbolically it means what is inside; household;[20] a family namely. In the normal course of worldwide societies, including Israel, the homes consisted of a husband, wife, children, and at times aged parents or unmarried family members. Not much different than modern times. Additionally, it means a place to lodge or a tent to dwell inside.[21] Placing tents together represents a tribe or a community of people. In the wilderness the Israelites were divided into twelve tribes and placed their tents around the Tent of Meeting according to their particular tribe and status of leadership.

Communities are represented by homes and buildings and the strength of community can be revealed by the number and size of these buildings. But the most important remembrance of this letter is what is inside the tent or house. What is the spiritual and emotional atmosphere inside the family home? God yearns to dwell among His people which includes the home whether it be a tent or permanent structure. Is it a home of shalom or peace or a home with questionable behavior? We want to work hard at building the home, whether it be a tent or house, into a habitation where God will be welcome.

> *"I heard a loud voice from the throne say, "See! God's Sh'khinah is with mankind, and he will live with them. They will be his people, and he himself, God-with-them, will be their God" (Revelation 21:3).*

The letter "Bet" is used in Hebrew words such as *"ha-bayit ha-rishon"* which means, "The first Temple" or *"beit;'av"* which means family, clan or house of the father."[22] Nations are built with the family units who dwell in portable or permanent structures.

Trust is foundational to a marriage between a man and a woman whose marriage is ordained by God. The home must have trust as one of the foundational stones. This kind of marriage for a man, who has found the blessing of a godly woman, realizes his trust is from within his heart and it will be proven she is a great asset to him. Why does a husband trust her? She has gained his confidence by her fear of God and her ability to lead the home with spiritual and physical strength. Trusting her from his heart means he has trusted the Lord to give him a trustworthy wife. She works to build a home starting with the truth of the Bible. The home is only of great value if the husband can trust his wife from his deepest place of passion and emotion which is his spirit.

The home is only of intrinsic value if the husband can trust his wife with his whole heart.

The home is a representation as a dwelling in relation to the "Tent of Meeting" as taught in the book of Exodus and Leviticus. As the Tabernacle of God was a place of dwelling and habitation, it also was a place of revelation of God's tremendous love for His family the Israelites. He dwelt among His bride.

Worth noting, the first Hebrew letter written in the Torah is "Bet". The creation story reveals a loving Father, Son, and Spirit, who builds a good home for mankind. The earth and its fullness was good and well designed for mankind. It was designed by God to build healthy familial relationships and these future generations, propagated by a husband and wife, will need a father who relies and has confidence in his spouse. He is reassured his faithful wife will be able to achieve her task at hand, just as the apostle Paul was confident with the church of Galatia. *(See Galatians 5:7-10.)*

King Y'hoshafat trusted God in his heart *(See 2Chronicles 17:1-6)*. A husband can and should be able to trust his "love" from his deepest seat of emotions, feelings, passions and thoughts. The wife has won a place in the inner-most being of a husband's spiritual existence because in her heart she has highly regarded the Lord and His ways. He has tested her devotion and it has proved to show she is fit to be a great gain and asset to the home. Her testimony among her peers will be valuable as a witness to Yeshua the Savior and His love. A true capable wife does not employ flattering talk or a false front but rather she is a women who has been embraced by God spiritually, in order to be oriented toward and into building His kingdom upon the earth starting with the home.

> *But so what? All that matters is that in every way, whether honestly or in pretense, the Messiah is being proclaimed; and in that I rejoice. Yes, and I will continue to rejoice, for I know that this will work out for my deliverance, because of your prayers and the support I get from the Spirit of Yeshua the Messiah. It all accords with my earnest expectation and hope that I will have nothing to be ashamed of; but rather, now, as always, the Messiah will be honored by my body, whether it is alive or dead. (Philippians 1:18-20).*

She is not just an asset or a gain to her husband. She is a great asset and a great gain to her husband and family household! Her greatness is achieved by her servant-hood to the Almighty. *(See Matthew 20:24-28.)* Ultimately she has given her whole life to the

Lord and not her husband. In turn, as the years pass, the Lord will honor her as He brings her comfort. *(See Psalms 71:18-21.)*

This proverb takes time. Trust from a husband's heart is established by the wife as she proves herself loving and loyal to her husband. True greatness of a marriage is a creation of God for a blessing to the home. But the husband and wife have stewardship over this blessing. Having such a wife will prove to be a great advantage and give him a sense of victory by winning her affection for a lifetime of happiness and bliss.

True greatness of a marriage is a creation of God for a blessing to the home.

Living a life of riches and material blessing is meaningless without having a wife that can surpass this material bounty. She will demonstrate herself to be a great asset to the home. Not a lifetime of liability. Due to her love and worship of God, blessings will follow her into the home where her blessed husband resides. He will want to come home for love and rest that is expressed by his wife.

Just before the last Passover that Yeshua Messiah would celebrate and prior to sacrificing Himself for the sins of mankind, He spoke those wonderful words concerning a home to His disciples that we find in *John 14:1-2*,

> *"Don't let yourselves be disturbed. Trust in God and trust in me. In my Father's house are many places to live...."*

Our Savior is preparing a home to receive His bride which is the church or congregation of saints. He is preparing a useful "Beit" (house) which is a covering or structure. In heaven there are buildings such as mansions, synagogues, and restaurants. The New Jerusalem is being constructed and the Apostle John saw it in a vision completed as described in the book of Revelation. But the value is in who will dwell in the buildings.

> *"Then I saw a new heaven and a new earth, for the old heaven and the old earth had passed away, and the sea was no longer there. Also I saw the holy city, New Yerushalayim coming down out of heaven from God, prepared like a bride beautifully dressed for her husband"* **(Revelation 21:1-2)**.

In the book of Ephesians we see the love our Messiah has for His future wife as He, one day, will receive her into His eternal home. We find these words in *Ephesians 5:25-27*,

> *"As for husbands, love yours wives, just as the Messiah loved the Messianic Community, indeed, gave Himself upon its behalf, in order to set it*

apart for God, making it clean through immersion in the mikveh, so to speak, in order to present the Messianic Community to Himself as a bride to be proud of, without a spot, wrinkle or any such thing, but holy and without defect."

This is the example we have for the home and what should be inside the house among a husband and wife. As he trusts her from his heart, the man will express his love to her, giving her the confidence of having a soulmate who believes in her. In this relationship of a capable trusting wife, her efforts will bring honor and dignity to her husband and home.

"His eyes were like a fiery flame, and on his head were many royal crowns" (Revelation 19:12a)

Let Us Reason Together

What blessings has God planted in your marriage?

How does a godly marriage resemble the ultimate wedding with the church as the bride of Yeshua?

What is the value of trust in your relationship?

What questions, thoughts or feelings do you have after reading chapter two?

NOTES

NOTES

NOTES

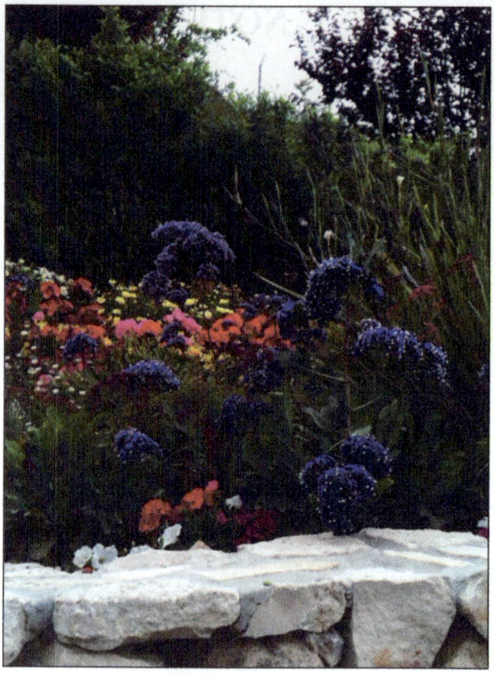

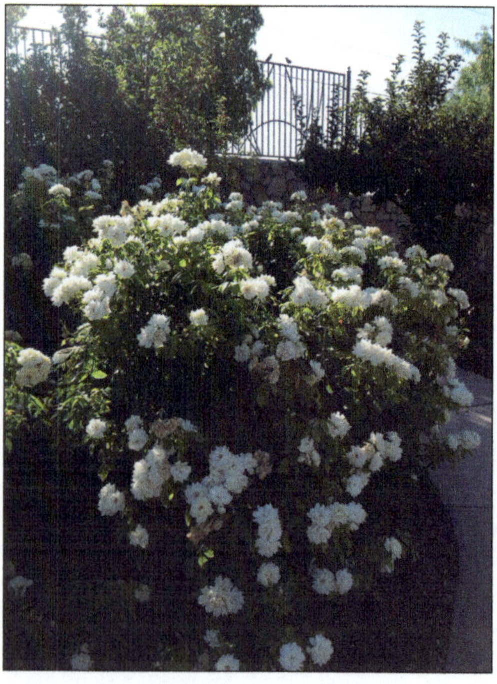

Chapter 3

SHE WORKS

"She works to bring him good, not harm, all the days of her life." (Proverbs 31:12)

The third letter of the Hebrew alphabet is called "*Gimmel*" (pronounced "gee-mel")and has the sound of a "g" as in "gift."[23] The pictographic shape represents the head of a camel lifted up.[24] Symbolically it represents; to lift up, or pride.[25] It could also mean a camel's hump as a reservoir of water for a long journey through a desert.[26] If you have observed camels standing around you will notice they lift up their heads and observe their surroundings. Lifting someone up to bring honor and dignity to them characterizes this letter "Gimmel" in this proverb. Exaltation takes effort with purpose. There is an underpinning reason why someone or something is being lifted up among others.

Hebrew words beginning with the letter "Gimmel" such as "*ge-vu-rot*" God's might, "*ge-dul-lah*" greatness, or "*ge-fen'emet*" the

True Vine, all connect in meaning as they use this letter to convey a message of truth. As we lift up the names of God and lift up Yeshua as the True Vine we bring Him praise, glory, and honor. He is mighty and great in exaltation. This is the work of the Holy Spirit. We, as believers, are to lift up and bring good to the name of God. Our lives are open written letters and we are the aroma of the Messiah (*See 2 Corinthians 2:14-15.*) We are not to bring harm but rather goodness to the family of God.

In this proverb, the noble wife works to advance and achieve goodness towards her husband. Her thoughts of love and devotion lead to active will and action to exalt her husband by her personal feelings of pleasure in her lifetime companion. Christ-like women want to honor and lift up their husbands to give them a true feeling of worth as a man. Her works are intentional and not under compulsion. She is free to act and think as she herself has gracefully demonstrated her ability to encourage and make a good reputation and name for her husband and ultimately, the whole family which can include extended members such as grandparents.

Her children and the community will take notice of a husband being lifted up among his peers.

Men love to be loved by their wives and they take much pleasure in a wife who is in love with them. A man's ego is enhanced if she is fulfilling to him with pleasure and passion of true protective love.

This will persuade and bring convincing proofs he is valuable and precious to her. Her children and the community will take notice of a husband being lifted up among his peers.

But there is also a difficult side of a wife bringing goodness to her husband. Sometimes this goodness is in the form of a rebuke, admonition, or verbal correction in order to maintain a husband's worthy status of honorable exaltation. In these moments of a resolute and brave wife, she is being used by the Holy Spirit. She truly wants to bring him good and not harm. Sometimes a stiff word of correction is needed to protect the family name. She must however, be extremely careful in the way this is done. It is never approached in a public environment or with a desire to humiliate him. God's word is steeped in correction with guidelines on the appropriate manner and timeliness.

If a husband is going through a difficult time such as a job loss, family crisis, or a spiritual low she can bring a recollection of past happiness and an assurance of eternal hope in Yeshua Messiah. Her comforting words of encouragement will continue all the days of her life in marriage. Even if she becomes a widow, her "love" will always be lifted up in honor and memory of past bygone days of a righteous marriage. The goodness she brings is the fruit of the Holy Spirit.

> *"But the fruit of the Spirit is love, joy, peace, patience, kindness, goodness, faithfulness, humility, self-control" (Galatians 5:22-23a).*

I believe, spiritually speaking, women are more inclined to bear the fruit of the Spirit than men are apt to do. That doesn't mean that being a man provides an excuse to dismiss the fruit of the Spirit. But walking in the fruit of the Spirit or oneness seems to come easier for women. The exegesis of this verse reveals fruit not fruits. The Holy Spirit expresses oneness in the fruit. Every metaphorical fruit listed works in harmony together at equal level. Co-equal fruit just as the Father, Son, and Spirit are co-equal. Living in this spiritual fruit helps to avoid bringing harm to a husband. At times, it is difficult for a female to deal with her husband in a host of circumstances. Her efforts to work hard at maintaining his good name requires the fullness of the Holy Spirit's wisdom.

The word harm in this proverb can mean evil speech, malicious gossip[27], or extravagant covetousness by an extreme desire for wealth and material gain. An ungrateful wife who is morally reprehensible and a violator of the Torah can and will bring great harm to a husband's reputation and financial status. Demoralizing a husband because of his financial situation, intellectual abilities, or not in keeping with a wife's expectation, can lead her to verbally assault and speak evil of his dignity in front of the family and friends. A noble wife will not commit such ungodly actions.

But rather an honorable and godly woman will want to bring her lover goodness instead of harm, all the days of her whole life. As she lives to worship the Lord by meditating upon the Scriptures, and ultimately giving God all the praise and exaltation, she will manifest righteousness and goodness towards her husband.

As she journeys through life and marriage there are going to be dry moments in the wilderness of this relationship. But, the Holy Spirit will guide and sustain her to achieve honor towards her husband. She is sustained by the spiritual reservoir of living water to lead her to give love and grace towards her husband. Her efforts bring honor and a lifting up of her husband in goodness which bring honor to God in praise and worship.

Yeshua said, in *John 12:32*,

> *"As for me, when I am lifted up from this earth, I will draw everyone to myself."*

This lifting up, which means His death on a Roman stake, was done for the good of mankind by a willful passionate loving God. His perfect works brings us good, not harm, if we believe in Him and trust in Him. This is the heart of the Father, in heaven. His Torah, which points to His only begotten Son, will bring goodness to man if we lift Him up through worship and the praises of Psalms.

> *"See how my servant will succeed! He will be raised up, exalted, highly honored" (Isaiah 52:13)*!

It is the duty of the Bride of Christ to exalt Yeshua by advancing the Gospel to its fullness, bringing goodness to a lost world of turmoil and confusion. This will open a pathway to the true worship of Almighty God. It ultimately brings goodness, not harm, to our future husband Yeshua Messiah. We are to do this all the days of our betrothal and eventually eternal marriage to Him as the Body of Christ.

> *"For when our Lord Yeshua returns, what will be our hope, our joy, our crown to boast about? Won't it be you? Yes, you are our glory and our joy."* *(1Thessalonians 2:19-20)*!

Let Us Reason Together

Who is the *best* wife that you may know?
What attributes give her this title?
What changes must you make in your life to become that woman?
As a husband, what steps do you need to take to share your thoughts with your wife?

What questions, thoughts, or feelings do you have after reading chapter three?

NOTES

NOTES

NOTES

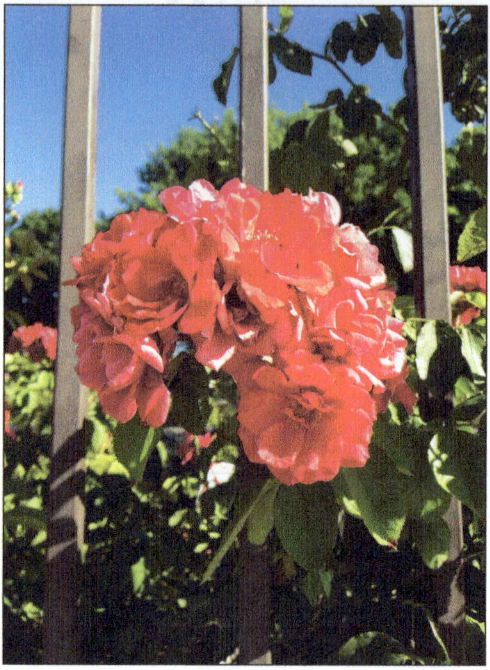

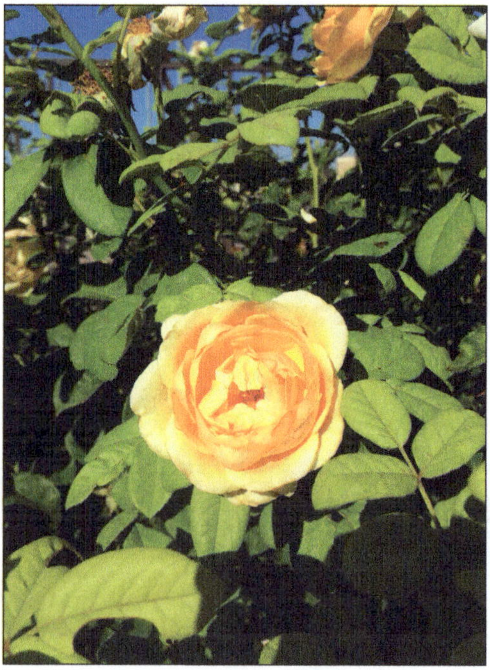

Chapter 4

SHE PROCURES

"She procures a supply of wool and flax and works with willing hands." (Proverbs 31:13)

"The fourth letter of the Hebrew alphabet is called *"Dalet"* (pronounced as "dah-let")."[28] It has the sound of "d" as in "door."[29] The original Paleo-Hebrew pictographic shape is a door[30] or "tent door."[31] Its symbolic meaning is "pathway, or enter."[32] We spend our lives constantly entering or exiting doors. Whether literal or spiritual we enter or exit for a reason. A female is a door to this life on earth. Every human born on earth had to pass through a mother's body. Doors whether they are made from animal skin, cloth for tents, or wood and metal for doors on buildings are controlled entry and exit points. A house would be useless without doors being part of the structure.

This letter is easily applied in conceptual thoughts about a woman. She can be a door or a pathway to receiving blessings from God. This is due to a motivated wife who cares about her household and those who enter or exit the doors to her home. As one enters a home with a woman of valor and love of the Lord, the spiritual atmosphere is a result of Gods blessings entering through her spirit. She is a vessel of honor that has an opening to receive God's spiritual gifts of the Spirit which can later be poured out upon others from the same opening.

"Dalet" signifies a pathway or the way to true worship. The true religion of entering into worship of God will be manifested by a wife and mother who really does want to devote herself to help support and provide the necessities of life for her husband, children and servants in the home. She can be a door and path to the true financial strength of the home and community.

Hebrew words that use the letter "Dalet" such as *"de-vir"*; Holy of Holies, "d*a-var*"; Word or *"din"* describing justice,[33] all convey a pathway to life. The Holy of Holies could only be seen by entering a tent door. God's Word is a pathway to eternal life and justice is a pathway to a civilized orderly society.

Is it any wonder a female is given, by God, the ability to be a door or pathway to representing Him? As the Lord helps a father provide and care for his children, so too, a wife, works to supervise and care for the needs of the family unit. She too is a pathway to the love, nurturing and health of the home.

In this proverb her first door of defense against poverty is to procure a supply of wool and flax with care and effort. Her perceptive skills at carefully choosing the finest of wool and flax at a good price is a pathway to meeting the clothing needs of the family and eventually a source of textile income. A capable wife will test and touch the wool looking for the crimp, color, and diameter of the fiber. She seeks out the strength of the wool knowing stress causes a sheep or goat to grow weak wool. This wool will match her character which is strong, beautiful and fine.

A supply of flax and wool used to make cloth and linen gives her the necessary resources to secure a stockpile of cloth. This economic foresight is going to be an avenue to her immediate future of entrepreneurship. Linen, garments and rugs are going to be made from this wool and flax.

The wife's positive approach to work with willing hands is a godly example and an open door to her children's education which results in them becoming productive citizens of society.

Another quality of a valuable wife is her zeal to work with willing hands. Her educated mind has opened a door to business economics that requires eagerness and a resolute passion for movement and action. When a capitalistic profit is available to those converting raw materials to textile products, the result is motivation and hard labor. She has entered the door of opportunity that can have a huge impact on the financial security of her home. God has ordained in His Word that those who work with willing hands and use their wisdom can enter a door of prosperity spiritually and physically.

I have personally witnessed women in and around my life work with willing effort in order to help provide the necessary finances to secure my education especially Bible school. The wife's positive approach to work with willing hands is a godly example and an open door to her children's education which results in them becoming productive citizens of society. The fact is, the wealth of a home can provide better education opportunities than one that controlled by slothful and lazy parents.

"Also, make it your ambition to live quietly, to mind your own business and to earn your living by your own efforts-just as we told you." (1 Thessalonians 4:11)

I believe hard work to care for your children will open the door for conversations about God and His Holy word to the children first and then with those whom you come into social contact. If she takes care of the immediate physical needs, she develops an audience who is prone to listen to her words. Don't talk about your love, show me! Show me your eagerness to care and feed me and I will listen to what God has laid on your heart about me and His anointed Scripture. Every person who shows practical care for me, can share God's word with me. Her hard work and a brilliant mind can open a pathway to building a better future for her husband, children and community. This extends far past the physical needs into the emotional and spiritual as well.

Yeshua the Christ is the perfect representation of a door or pathway. He cares for us and He works continuously on our behalf. He's building a future and eternal home for His Bride. This includes open doors to the spiritual world and eventually an eternal home with the Father. This required willing action and effort on the part of Yeshua. He obeyed His Father and it gave His disciples an open door of reception. Faith and trust in the Lord will allow the believers to enter the open path to everlasting life.

> *"For I know what plans I have in mind for you, 'says Adonai, 'plans for well-being, not for bad things; so that you can have hope and a future." (Jeremiah 29:11)*

He sits before the Father working to secure a place for His beloved. This place is the New Jerusalem with twelve gates as described in the book of Revelation. These are open entryways for only the believing and faithful people of the Lord. Our approach to these gates are dependent on The Way which is Yeshua the Messiah.

> *"But because He lives forever, His position as cohen does not pass on to someone else; and consequentially, he is totally able to deliver those who approach God through Him; since he is alive forever and thus forever able to intercede on their behalf." (Hebrews 7:24-25)*

He zealously works even today in heaven on our behalf. He is the true Door of life. He is the pathway to our eternal hope with our Father.

He willingly works among people, individuals, and holds the righteous close to his heart.

God's work does not cease. He willingly works among people, individuals, and holds the righteous close to his heart. He has given his Son the ministry of reconciliation which opens the door to eternal life for those who believe and trust in Him.

> *"But He answered them, "My Father has been working until now, and I too am working." (John 5:17)*

Today the Lord Almighty is working to secure the Jewish people in Israel as He did during the Exodus story. During the wilderness wandering God worked to build Israel's religious worship in Truth, established tribal authority and organized civil law. He worked to prepare Israel to enter the pathway to the Promised Land. God opened the door for Israel to enter His Shabbat rest.

God's main work are His acts of salvation to believing Israel and all believing Gentiles (**See Habakkuk 2:4.**) His goal is to unite all people as one in Yeshua Messiah. The church's mission today is God's willing active work to bring all the lost through the Door which is Yeshua Messiah. This is achieved with those believers who work with willing hands in order to gain and share the necessary finances enabling the Gospel to be taught around the whole world.

> *"Thus says Adonai, the Holy One of Isra'el, his Maker:" You ask for signs concerning my children? You give orders concerning the work of my hands? I am the one who made earth! I created human beings on it! I-my hands-stretched out the heavens, and directed all their number" (Isaiah 45:11-12).*

So too, God works through a wife and she is the motivational example for all women to work with intense willingness. Her labor done in faith and for the Lord can be a door to open blessings spiritually and economically for the family. In this she will reveal the vast wealth she carries within her passion and zeal.

> *"I am coming soon; hold on to what you have, so that no one will take away your crown." (Revelation 3:11)*

Let Us Reason Together

What door are you opening for others?

What door is being opened for you?

How intense is your willingness to complete your tasks of love?

What questions, thoughts, or feelings do you have after reading chapter four?

NOTES

NOTES

NOTES

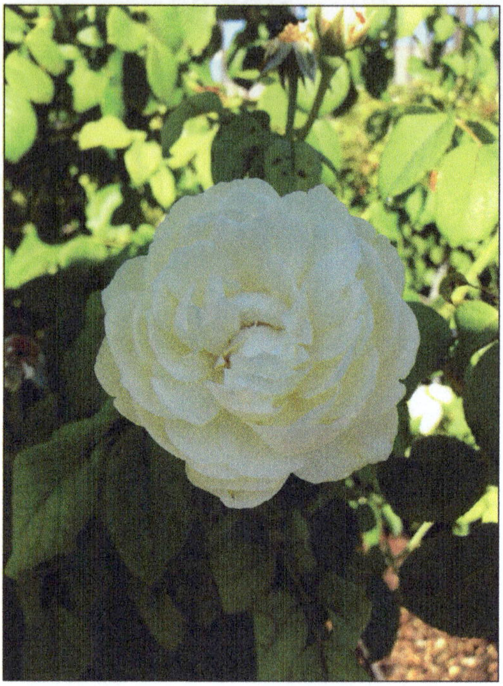

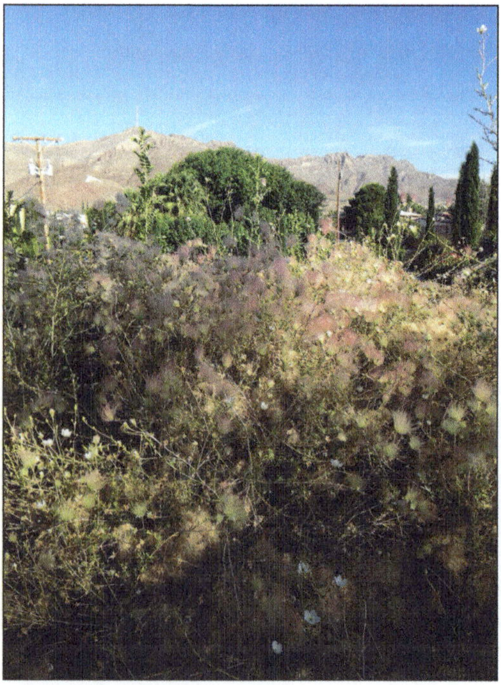

Chapter 5

SHE IS LIKE

"She is like those merchant vessels, bringing her food from far away." (Proverbs 31:14)

The fifth letter of the Hebrew alphabet is called "*Hey*" (pronounced "hey").[34] It has the sound "h" as in "hay."[35] The original pictographic shape represents a window, lattice,[36] or a "man raising his hands in prayer toward the sun."[37] The symbolic concepts are to reveal,[38] to behold,[39] or praising God.[40]

Hebrew words using "Hey" such as "*had-da-var*"; The Word, "*ho-sha`na*"; "O save!", or "*hal-lel*" praise songs,[41] all reveal revelations of God in what we can behold for salvation and relationship. Our whole existence with the Lord Almighty is based entirely upon His revelation of love to us and how we respond to Him in praise and worship. He opened heaven's window and allowed us to behold his eternal wonder, hence, the book of Revelation is a perfect example of the revelation of the Father, Son, and Holy Spirit.

In this proverb, it is a revealed detailed description of the practical wife's strong business characteristics. She has learned the economic ramification of maritime business and is likened to it. As a merchant vessel is a floating container with treasure and food from afar, so also is a women likened to a vessel. She is full of ideas, dreams and visions that are useful resources to the home and society.

She continually stocks the home with practical needs. Even though weather or famines come, she will struggle but succeed in getting the resources needed for the homes survival. So too, in the spirit, during times of tribulation or a spiritual dryness, she is ever seeking the Lord knowing her husband and children need her spirituals resources of hope, endurance, and faith in God.

One of the most magnificent sights to see is a ship with it sails up and in full bloom due to the winds. Especially when the ship is headed inland ready to download it treasures and food. People on the shore anticipate the arrival of food, new ideas, news, precious metals, diamonds, rubies, jewelry, clothing, animals, as well as new and interesting people.

Her work ethics contribute financially to the home and she is able and willing to go into the market place to bargain and barter in order to supply her home with great abundance. She knows where and how to shop for the sustenance of the children. She maintains the necessary supplies in good and bad times with a continual supply and storage of food. Her family praises God for her foresight and the husband brings her spoken honor for her loving care and concern.

She is never ending in bringing fresh food and products to the home. Always resourceful and thrifty when she shops and purchases.

She is like a spiritual window into heaven as the husband and children get a better understanding and view of God's care.

She is a spiritual vessel carrying the riches of Christ. Christ will be revealed in and through her in a practical way. She is a spiritual window into heaven as the husband and children get a better understanding and view of God's care and love.

> *"Oh the depth of the riches and the wisdom and knowledge of God! How unscrutable are his judgments! How unsearchable are his ways"* (**Romans 11:33**)!

God's riches and wisdom are unsearchable. He has to bring them to you. A noble wife is one of the vessels who like a merchant ship, brings spiritual truth from far away. She is an instrument of God who brings the glory of God to her family as she goes through life's journey in tempest-tossed waves. She is an anointed vessel whose sails are full of the Holy Spirit. She is an ambassador coming from afar to bring wisdom and revelation of God.

Just as ships arrived at port overfilled with their foreign cuisine so too a woman brings a host of heavenly emotions, knowledge, and prophecies of God to convey His wisdom and Word. This will give her a fulfilling purpose, as she joyfully works to please her God by working to meet the needs of the family both practically and spiritually. Behold this woman as we lift up holy hands and thank the Lord for her faithfulness to God and her home.

The most notable aspect of this proverb is the idea of her being a vessel metaphorically. The ships sails are useful if able to be guided by the winds for movement, so too a woman of a righteous spirit can catch the holy wind and be guided by the Spirit. She can be full of God's richest and best. The Apostle Paul was going to be such a vessel who carried the richness of Yeshua's love.

> *"But the Lord said to him, "Go, because this man is my chosen instrument to carry my name to the Goyim, even to their kings, and to the sons of Isra`el as well" (Acts 9:15).*

Yeshua is the perfect revelation of the letter "Hey". He is the window to the kingdom of heaven. His works of salvation reveal a loving Father who brings daily sustenance for all of mankind. Being perfectly filled with the Spirit, Yeshua was gifted to express the fruit and gifts of the Spirit. He is the ultimate merchant ship bringing his bride beautiful gifts of the Holy Spirit.

> *"On this mountain Adonai-Tzva'ot make for all peoples a feast of rich food and superb wines, delicious, rich food and superb, elegant wines" (Isaiah 25:6).*

We are blessed to read and one day see, by revealed prophecy, the wonders of the eternal love and care of Yeshua Messiah. This rich vessel is going to bring all the saints of God a wonderful and fulfilling feast. For all eternity, the supply will never run out.

So to, a virtuous wife is a living example of her Savior. Her abilities and skill can and will accomplish the practical and spiritual needs of the home. Every day brings the opportunity and the responsibility which includes the early morning hours.

> *"So, my brothers, whom I love and long for, my joy and my crown, my dear friends, keep standing firm in union with the Lord." (Philippians 4:1)*

Let Us Reason Together

What kind of vessel do you envision yourself to be? (A cruise ship, a sailboat, a two-masted schooner, a clipper, or a fluyt?
What cargo are you carrying to your family and friends?

What questions, thoughts, or feelings do you have after reading chapter five?

NOTES

NOTES

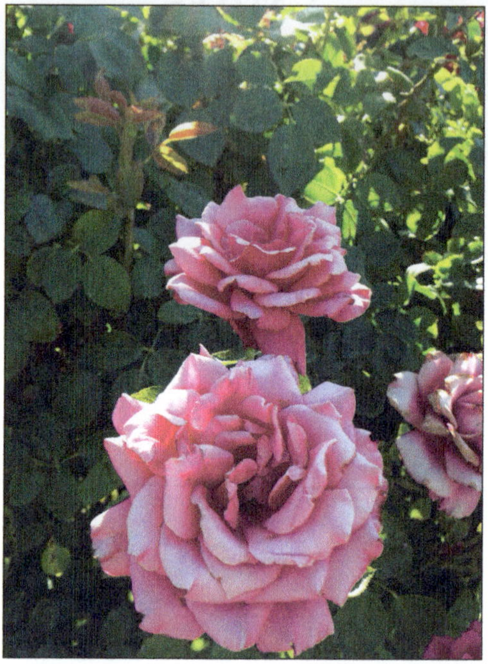

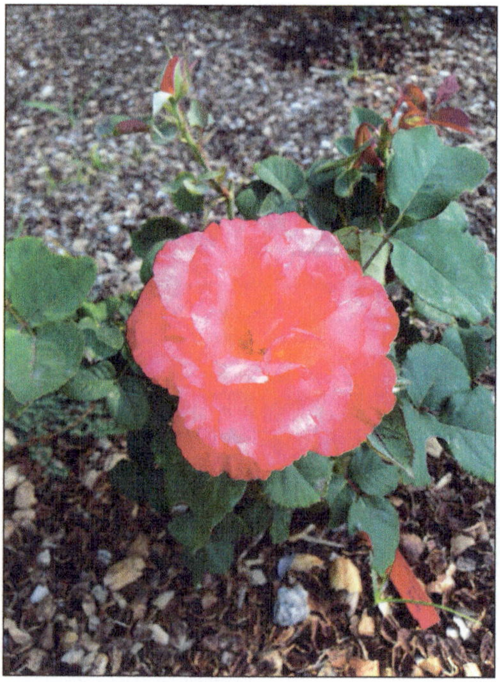

Chapter 6

IT'S STILL DARK

"It's still dark when she rises to give food to her household and orders to the young women serving her" (Proverbs 31:15).

The sixth letter of the Hebrew alphabet is called "*Vav*" (pronounced "vahv") and has the sound "v" as in "victory".[42] It's paleo-Hebrew shape depicts nail or peg.[43] The symbolic meaning is to "secure"[44] or to be "anchored."[45] Simply it means to add to or secure to a person, place, or thing.

A family needs a secure foundational home of health and rest from the previous day's activities. The home is a place to eat, fellowship, rest, and above all worship God. Adding value to the home is when one places their sure footing on the solid rock of God. Obedience to the woman of the home rests on the security established by her strength of leadership. Her leadership starts early each day and she is going to make sure her spiritual, mental and physical strength are going to be part of the equation as each new day arrives. Men who have not attached a virtuous woman, by a covenant vow of a lifelong union, are incomplete. The addition of a virtuous wife anchors a practical and godly spiritual condition in the home. The family's needs will be taken care of to the best of her ability as she trusts in the Lord.

Obedience to the woman of the home rests on the security established by her strength of leadership.

A Hebrew word using the letter "Vav" is *"vai-yiq-ra"* (Leviticus) which means "And He called."[46] This book details instructions on how the Hebrew nation is to anchor their honor of Yehovah. Adonai in His eternal wisdom, secured the necessary teachings on how to approach Him in worship. Men gained the confidence of a loving God who showed how to anchor their lives upon His Torah and not let go of Him. Even in the dark of night as the Hebrew nation rested in the wilderness, their Lover anchored His pillar of fire over them ensuring the Israelites that He was going to meet their need of food, water and safety. He secured His leadership among them. He was not going to let go of His children as they obeyed His commands. They, being lead into the wilderness, had to trust in their eternal Father to look ahead and provide nourishment to sustain their lives. As Israel's history unfolded, the Lord continued to add Holy Scripture to lead and guide them into the Promised Land in order to secure a place of care and rest.

Another Hebrew word using "Vav" is "vid-duy" which means "confession".[47] In order to secure a righteous relationship with the Lord we need to nail our sins on the cross. This is done by humble confession to our Father in an act of repentance. We can secure a right relationship to Yeshua, the One who took on our sins and was nailed to the wooden stake planted in rocky earthy soil. He rose early in the morning from a night of intense prayer and through His divine will He willingly gave up His arms and feet to be nailed to the altar of sacrifice in order to give those who believe in Him eternal security in heaven. Mankind could now have peace knowing they can have a home of spiritual rest and nourishment.

> *"Then Yeshua said to them, "Yes, indeed! I tell you that unless you eat the flesh of the Son of Man and drink his blood, you do not have life in yourselves. Whoever eats my flesh and drinks my blood has eternal life-that is, I will raise him up on the Last Day. For my flesh is true food, and my blood is true drink. Whoever eats my flesh and drinks my blood lives in me, and I live in him" (John 6:53-56).*

In this proverb, we see each day brings a host of routine and probable new challenges. It is early and still dark outside but her foresight will transcend upon the dawn of the day. She will rise up to begin encouraging the household with love and kindness. Everyone has rested, hopefully, and is in need of water and food. The wife of the home has plans for the day and household duties need to be accomplished so she can secure her business affairs. The sun has crested the horizon and orders are assigned among the servant girls. There is the transmission of command in order to see that everyone including the hired help is cleaned, fed, dressed and guided into the responsibilities of the coming day.

The direction, provision and administration by the wife gives everyone the security of love and edification to be successful. Her character is revealed as one of the love, patience and faith. She is not going to allow the day to be wasted by being non-responsive and lazy. Each day brings unknown challenges that are a test by the Lord.

> *"I, Adonai, search the heart; I test inner motivations; in order to give to everyone what his actions and conduct deserve" (Jeremiah 17:10).*

Her husband watches the domestic affairs in operation. He is encouraged that provision to the home is secured and this gives him a sense of joy and happiness for his wife. Her sacrifice and worship to the Lord destroys laziness and irresponsibility. Her domestic affairs reveal a spiritual fortitude.

> *"But you, brothers, are not in the dark, so that the Day should take you by surprise like a thief; for you are all people who belong to the light, who belong to*

the day. We don't belong to the night or to darkness, so let's not be asleep, like the rest are; on the contrary, let us stay alert and sober" (*1 Thessalonians 5:4-6*).

The spiritual aspect of this practical parable is inexhaustible. Yeshua Messiah is the perfect representation of "Vav" as He too has provided the spiritual food and nourishment we all need. He loves us, and is ever watching over us as He sits at the right hand of our Father in heaven (***Mark 16:19***).

He so cares and loves us and is always there to meet our physical and spiritual needs and is ever interceding on our behalf to the Father. After His resurrection when He went up to Galilee, the disciples who were fishing, recognized Him from their boat when they saw Him on the shore (***John 21:1-14***). Yeshua was preparing food to meet their needs and He also gave them a catch of fish to meet their obligations to their home. He is a true mother at heart.

Yeshua the Savior of the world is not going to ever let go of you. He has secured eternally a home for you. Believers can anchor their eternity on their faith in Him. He wants all of His own to feel a sense of security knowing their spiritual and physical needs will be met in preparation for the coming day.

So also, a spiritually righteous wife knows her inward passion for her family and she also is an anchor for the home. Her zeal to help meet the needs of the family is a weapon against poverty and want.

"Thoughtless people inherit folly, but the cautious are crowned with knowledge." (Proverbs 14:18)

Let Us Reason Together

How has Yeshua provided for you most recently? How did you thank Him?

Think back to how He took care of the Israelites and provided for their needs. The same Father took care of them just as He cares for you today. What are your current needs?

In what areas might you be wasting precious time?

What steps can you take to resolve this situation?

What questions, thoughts, or feelings do you have after reading chapter six?

NOTES

NOTES

NOTES

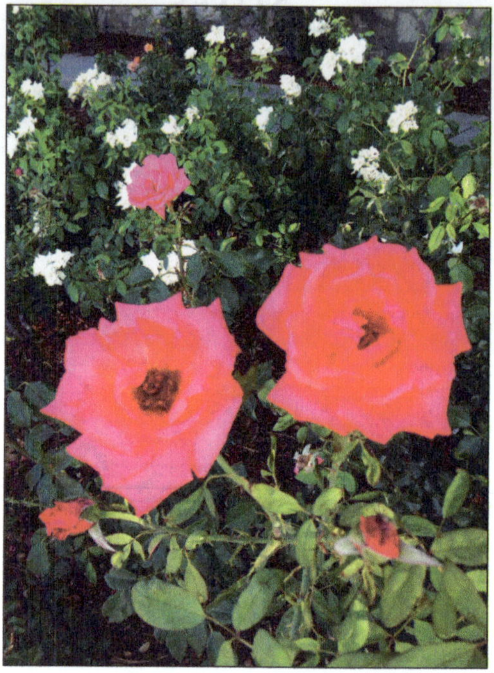

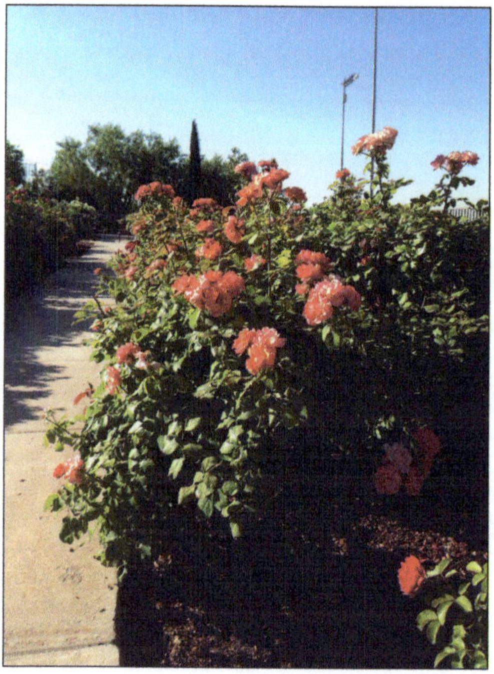

Chapter 7

SHE CONSIDERS

"She considers a field, then buys it, and from her earnings she plants a vineyard." (Proverbs 31:16)

"The seventh letter of the Hebrew alphabet is called *"Zayin"* (pronounced "zah-yeen").[48] It has the sound of "z" as in "zion."[49] Its paleo-Hebrew shape represents a weapon,[50] or plow.[51] The symbolic meaning is to cut, or cut off.[52]

A weapon can be used to protect. A knife was also instrumental in cutting covenant with God through offering sacrificial animals by shedding their blood through cutting. Avraham (Abraham) also cut covenant with God by the rite of circumcision. Through obeying the Lord, Avraham permanently established a relationship to the Lord (*See Genesis 17:9-14*). God gave him and his descendants through Yitz`chak (Isaac) and Ya`akov (Jacob) the Promised Land but again, this required the shedding of blood to cut or affirm the relationship and promises. A blood covenant was established by cutting off a portion of the flesh.

> *"Here is my covenant, which you are to keep, between me and you, along with your descendants after you; every male among you is to be circumcised" (Genesis 17:10).*

Hebrew words using "Zayin" such as "zik-ka-ron"[53]; "remembrance" or "ze-khar-yah"; meaning "God has remembered"[54] gives us insight into how God remembers His people by a cutting of a covenant with His Word and will.

In this proverb, when a woman commits herself to a man in marriage she is in a covenant relationship. In this union she is used as a mighty weapon against missed opportunities and poverty. She desires to partner in helping the financial stability of the home and is an active partner in this relationship. Her knowledge and skills will help build financial security for the home alongside with her husband. Her intellectual ingenuity will lead her to taking the land of Israel and benefiting from the covenant established between God and Israel. She will work the land and have the trust that faith in God will give the increase due to her obedience to Him.

Once her home is established and organized, her character of a shrewd business women begins to take shape. It is probably as a child she picked up on the responsibilities of husbandry. She has

She Considers

cultivated in her agrarian education the ability of growing crops and having the courage and foresight to conserve and manage a business in farming. Females as well as males worked the soil of Israel and tended the herds of sheep and goats. Harvest season needed all the family members to help during the short period of time to harvest the crops. She knows by experience it will be a challenge to raise food for a hopeful harvest and a profit.

She is thinking and contemplating upon the idea of buying a field, seeing it's potential earnings in which she is successful and seizing the opportunity, as a weapon, to protect her increase by investing in planting a vineyard. Her covenantal relationship to God and her husband drives her fortitude in land and farming techniques.

Her mind has been directed prudently, by not neglecting present duties, to grasp the idea she can purchase a field at a good price with the confidence of trusting the Lord for an increase. Her profits are not wasted on licentious living but are used in a wiser investment. From contemplation to action she has proven to her husband she has the ability to own and operate a business from the productive soil of Israel provided by God.

With her hands dry and bleeding, a vineyard is planted. I'm sure her children and servants were all involved in planting the vineyard. Her beauty and feminine qualities are set aside as she tackles the weather, rocks, hard soil, and probably ridicule from the envious. She's not looking for a hobby but rather she wisely uses her time to increase her family's financial strength through investment.

She's not looking for a hobby but rather she wisely uses her time to increase her family's financial strength through investment.

This proverb teaches a wife and mother can run a household and start a business by thoughtful consideration and support from her husband. Her brave spirited character knows no limit and she sees a world to conquer by using her knowledge in business through wise investment opportunities.

> *"His master said to him, 'Excellent! You are a good and trustworthy servant. You have been faithful with a small amount, so I will put you in charge of a large amount. Come and join in your master's happiness'" (Matthew 25:21)*!

Her earnings of increase will be used to pay God's tithe. This continues to establish worship and the teachings of God's Torah. Some of her money is used to buy sacrificial animals on behalf of herself and the family. Her shrewd godly business skills are a pathway to the shedding of sacrificial blood which continues the foreshadowed covenantal relationship to God.

She is using her ability to increase the kingdom of God, which revealed, is the Gospel of Yeshua. This Good News is the covenant through the shed blood of Yeshua Messiah that takes away the sin of the world and brings spiritual and physical blessings of prosperity.

This is a cycle of obedience and blessings. Through her faithfulness, God will bless the land and its fruit. God promised to causes the rains to come at the right time so she can be successful in raising crops to feed and prosper the family. Bless God and in turn the husband and children are blessed. Faith in God, hard work, a business head and wise thriftiness all combine for practical success.

Hard work, a business head and wise thriftiness all combine for practical success.

This proverb also reveals spiritual realities in Yeshua Messiah. Through the shedding of His blood, through weapons used to cut Him off from Israel, believers were purchased and cultivated by pruning to spiritually produce more believers for the kingdom of God.

> *"...The fact is, you don't belong to yourselves; for you were bought at a price. So use your bodies to glorify God " (I Corinthians 6:19b-20).*

Practical living can be used to glorify the Lord in the spiritual realm. As a woman, it is important to initiate your brave spirit into a spiritual weapon. Do not let the enemy cut you off from the inward yearning to prove your nobility in the area of business. Poverty and economic hardship leads to spiritual digression. You are rich in Yeshua Messiah. But, it comes only with perseverance, courage, and the understanding that in yourself you are weak but He, Yeshua, is a mighty weapon. We read in *John 15:1-4*,

> *"I am the real vine, and my Father is the gardener. Every branch which is part of me but fails to bear fruit, he cuts off; and every branch that does bear fruit, he prunes, so that it may bear more fruit. Right now, because of the word which I have spoken to you, you are pruned. Stay united with me, as I will with you-for just as the branch can't put forth fruit by itself apart from the vine, so you can't bear fruit apart from me".*

She is a woman that has cultivated her spirit in the good soil, the Torah. She bears the fruit of the Living Word and her relationship, by a bloody covenant to God, is blessed as He prunes any unfruitful branches in her life which could be oppression by men or self-pity.

This proverb also rises above the realm of a wife assisting her husband economically. It's about the spiritual investment of a woman in God's vineyard. This will build a strong wall around the home.

> *"You crown the year with your goodness, your tracks overflow with richness." (Psalms 65:12(11))*

<u>Let Us Reason Together</u>

Where do you spend more of your time? Licentious living or working on wiser investments?

What were the last useless branches that God pruned from your life? How did you feel initially?

What was the outcome of the pruning experience?

As a husband, what thoughtful consideration are you offering your wife to ensure her success?

What questions, thoughts, or feelings do you have after reading chapter seven?

NOTES

NOTES

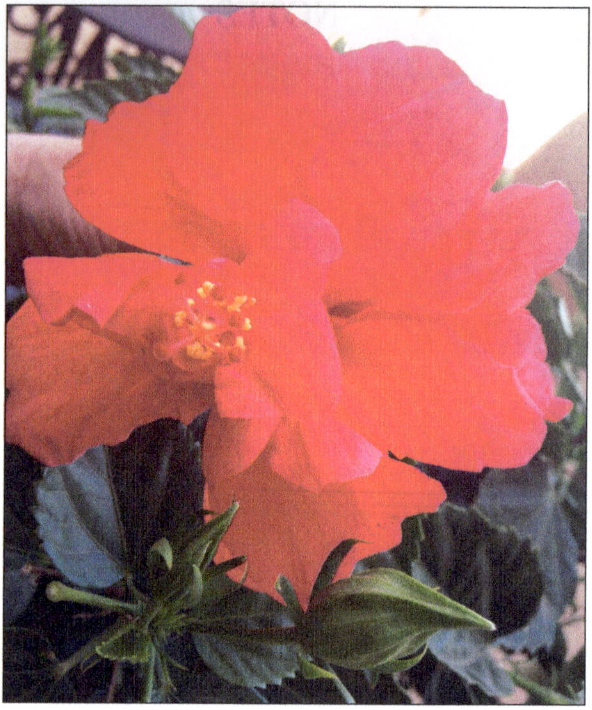

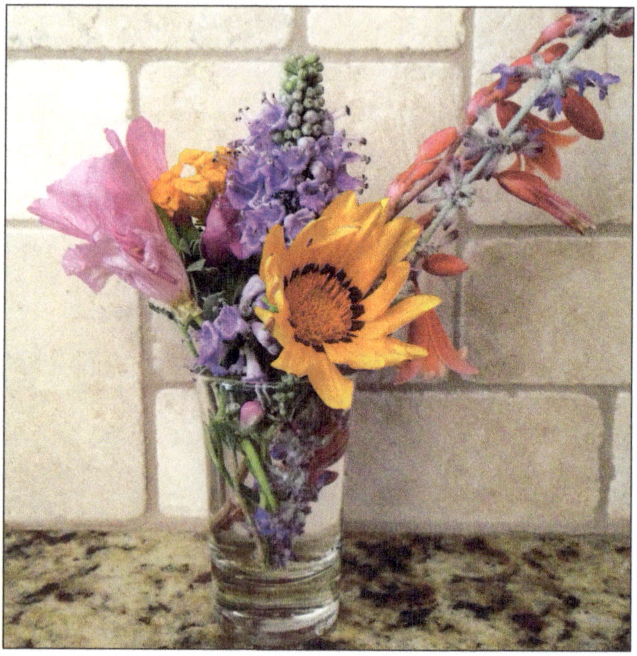

Chapter 8

SHE GATHERS

"She gathers her strength around her and throws herself into her work." (Proverbs 31:17)

The eighth letter of the Hebrew alphabet is called "Chet" (rhymes with "let") and is pronounced by lightly scraping the throat when sounding the "ch" as in "Bach".[55] You have to use your throat to pronounce the beginning of the letter not the front of your tongue and teeth. Its original pictographic shape is tent wall,[56] fence, or a chamber.[57] Its symbolic meaning is private,[58] separate,[59] to protect.[60] It conveys to keep in or keep out.

The concept is a fence to protect or building a wall to isolate from chaos and to keep order. An excellent concept of separating dimensions to keep in or keep out is found in the book of Psalms.

"By your strength you split the sea in two, in the water you smashed sea monsters' heads, you crushed the

heads of Livyatan and gave it as food to the creatures of the desert. You cut channels for springs and streams, you dried up rivers that had never failed. The day is yours, and the night yours; it was you who established light and sun. It was you who fixed all the limits of the earth, you made summer and winter" (**Psalms 74:13-17**).

Everything created has boundaries that surround and separate. Hebrew words using "Chet" such as "*cha-viv*"; beloved, "*cha-ver*"; comrad, "*chag*"; festival, or "*cha-zut*"; prophecy,[61] all reveal eternal implications for what is valuable to separate oneself from in order to achieve a personal Christ-like relationship as ordained by the Father. For example, the festivals of the Lord (**Leviticus 23**) bring fellow believers together who share God's love in word and way as they surround each other singing psalms and hymns to the Lord. They, our fellow saints, are like protecting walls that are useful boundaries which prevail over the enemy and keep us from straying spiritually.

Even the Torah, which is the revelation of Yeshua as the Savior of mankind, is a wall of spiritual protection that creates intimacy with the Father. It sets boundaries that can build spiritual walls of truth and protection from the enemies of God, whether spiritual or physical. The establishment of boundaries has two well defined purposes. The first is to keep the unwanted out of your personal space but the second keeps you from escaping and running amuck out in the world where you don't belong. God's Word provides a vast frontier of freedom for those who know Him intimately.

In this proverb, she is preparing to set out at task like a soldier. As a soldier girds themselves with necessary weaponry and equipment, so too this noble woman is going to gird herself with strength spiritually, mentally and physically. Strength will surround her loins and hips. The arms and shoulders began to complete the task by her will to be steadfast, steady, reliable and unwavering. She has trained to stand her ground and eventually secure enemy territory.

Her dedication and zealousness reveals her willingness to do battle against the domestic requirements outside business affairs.

Her actions of labor and love reveal a woman to be reckoned with. Her dedication and zealousness reveals her willingness to do battle against the domestic requirements outside business affairs. Her physical demonstration represents her mental and especially spiritual war of will. I watched my mother live out her last years in pain. She did her best to help with our homes domestic care. But my most amazing memory of her was when she would play the piano in worship to God. I knew it was painful for her body as she moved her arms across the piano keys. This was a testimony to all of the saints who watched her worship God even in the most trying circumstances.

The Torah has revealed the importance of believers endeavoring to gather the strength of the Lord as they zealously go about the

Father's business. Her husband does not have to worry about her or go look for her to see what she is doing. He knows she is about her business with all her strength and might. Just like Yeshua He was about his Father's business wholeheartedly. We read these words in ***Luke 2:49***,

"He said to them,"Why did you have to look for me? Didn't you know that I had to be concerning myself with my Father's affairs?"

Yeshua separated himself from his earthly father and mother and surrounded Himself with His Father's house. He astonishing religious leaders with His spiritual interpretation of the Torah. He is a fortified city with a wall of bronze (***Jeremiah 1:18-19***). His ministry had practical responsibilities with spiritual implications.

A woman needs righteousness and strength as she accomplishes daily chores. But they are not done begrudgingly and in bitterness. She is grateful for what she has and makes the best of the routine by powering through any resistance whether in spirit, mind, or body. The husband see's this active woman and honors her hard work as she separates herself from idleness which can lead to sin.

*"It is God who girds me with strength; He makes my way go straight" (**Psalms 18:33(32)**).*

This is to be the belief of a noble woman. Her Savior is the perfect example of one who girds himself appropriately as he is separated to be holy and blameless before the Father.

"Justice will be the belt around His waist, faithfulness the sash around His hips" (Isaiah 11:5).

When spiritual warfare is required, Yeshua girds Himself and goes into battle on our behalf. He surrounds the situation and protects His own accordingly. So too, a righteous woman rolls up her sleeves gathering her spiritual strength from the living Torah and throws herself vigorously into prayer and Torah confession as she separates herself and goes into the inner chamber of spiritual intimacy and prayer with the Lord. We find these words in *1 Peter 4:11*,

"If someone speaks, let him speak God's words; if someone serves, let him do so out of strength that God supplies; so that in everything God may be glorified through Yeshua the Messiah-to Him be glory and power forever and ever. Amen."

The most infamous passage of Scripture concerning separating oneself for spiritual war to do battle is found in *Ephesians 6:11-18*. It describes a believer girding themselves with the truth of God's Word for spiritual war. This girding represents one who surrounds themselves with truth for added spiritual protection and says,

"Use all the armor and weaponry that God provides, so that you will be able to stand against the deceptive tactics of the Adversary. For we are not struggling against human beings, but against the rulers, authorities and cosmic powers governing this darkness, against the spiritual forces of evil in the heavenly realm. So take up every piece of war equipment God provides; so that when the evil day comes, you will be able to resist; and when the battle is won, you will still be standing. Therefore, stand! Have the belt of truth buckled around your waist, put on righteousness for a breastplate, and wear on your feet the readiness that comes from the Good News of shalom. Always carry the shield of trust, with which you will be able to extinguish all the flaming arrows of the Evil One. And take the helmet of deliverance; along with the sword given by the Spirit, that is, the Word of God; as you pray at all times, with all kinds of prayers and requests, in the Spirit, vigilantly and persistently, for all God's people."

<u>Her strength can be used spiritually as she surrounds herself with God's Torah and prays for His protection to keep out the enemy in her home.</u>

In the natural this blessed woman musters the strength to accomplish what is necessary for the home. But there is a spiritual reflection that is revealed. Her strength can be used spiritually as she surrounds herself with God's Torah and prays for His protection to keep out the enemy in her home. Ministry in the Spirit is work, but it is imperative that you, as a woman, prepare spiritually, emotionally, and physically as you embark on the given responsibilities always knowing the enemy attempts to destroy you and your efforts.

> *"How blessed is the man who perseveres through temptation! For after he has passed the test, he will receive as his crown the Life which God has promised to those who love him." (James 1:12)*

Let Us Reason Together

What are you doing battle against?

Plan out the steps you need to take to build your offensive line against the evil one.

Which verses provide spiritual strength? Emotional comfort? Physical peace and promises?

What questions, thoughts, or feelings do you have after reading chapter eight?

NOTES

NOTES

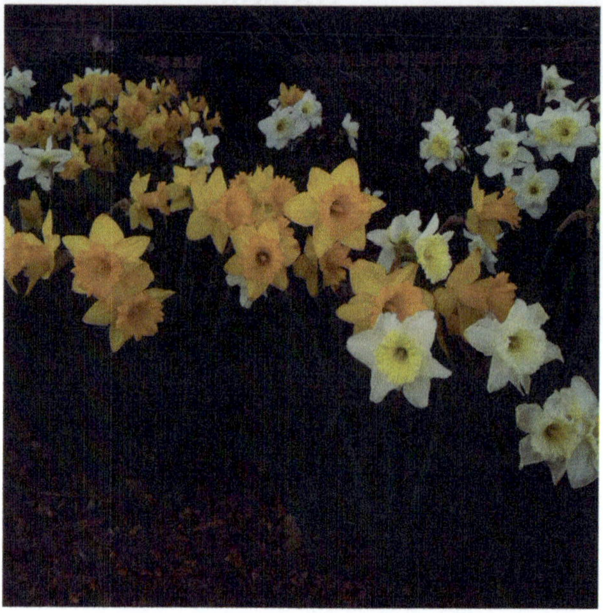

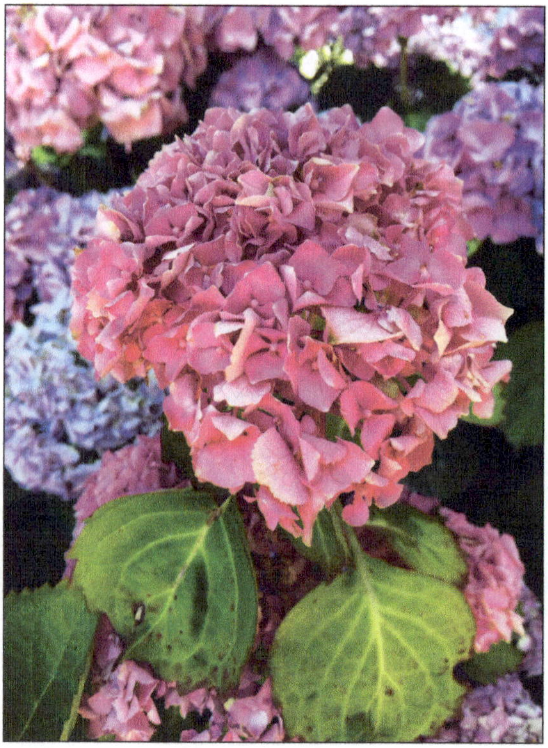

Chapter 9

SHE SEES

"She sees that her business affairs go well; her lamp stays lit at night." Proverbs 31:18

The ninth letter of the Hebrew alphabet is called "*Tet*" (rhymes with "met") and has the sound of "t" as in "talk".[62] The pictorial shape is "to twist, a snake,"[63] or "a basket."[64] Its symbolic meaning is, "to surround."[65]

This letter has a negative connotation as well as a positive one. The negative is the fact that the enemy surrounds us like a snake squeezing the life out of the unsuspecting or to bring fear, chaos and defilement to the family unit, community and nation. Eventually it can and will lead to death whether spiritually, mentally or physically.

But the positive characteristics of "T*et*" is the fact that a women, due to her gifting by the Lord, can surround her husband and children with righteousness in the spirit, prayer as a warrior, or confidence in the Lord Almighty. She knows the Lord has surrounded her home by His answer to prayer for love, security and protection. The spiritual victory is due to her faith in Yeshua, as Protector of the home.

<u>She knows the Lord has surrounded her home by His answer to prayer for love, security and protection.</u>

Hebrew words that use the letter "Tet" such as "tal-lit"; which is a prayer shawl, "ta-hor"; meaning clean; pure; innocent, or even "ta-ho-rot"; uncleanliness or ceremonial defilement[66] reveal there are spiritual and physical realities that surround everyone which can be a blessing or a curse to their lives. The tallit or prayer shawl is my endearing memory of being the first object that impacted my life as a believer in Yeshua Messiah. It is an amazing experience to don the prayer shawl surrounding the upper head and shoulders with this cloth. One can feel surrounded by the Lord in prayer and intimacy. The colors of the shawl and the meaning of the tassels on the four corners surrounding the worshiper reveal how the Lord surrounds his people symbolically and as a remembrance not to violate His Torah in word, interpretation and deed.

The wife of a home can have a huge impact on the lives of her husband, children, domestic helpers, and even society. She is a discerning woman whose spirit and mind are surrounded by the Lord's will and wisdom. Her wisdom brings her to a level as a tireless businesswoman. Even Yeshua likened Himself to a prudent and zealous accountant. We read these words in *Luke 15:8*,

"Another example: what women, if she has ten drachmas and loses one of these valuable coins, won't light a lamp, sweep the house and search all over until she finds it?"

In this proverb, we discover a housewife's work is never done. Especially in a prosperous home that requires, at often times, the necessity to burn the olive oil at night due to the end of the daylight hours. Her business opportunities prevent financial surrounding calamity in the home and the lamp may be required to lengthen "the daylight" in order to finish "quarterly reports" or finish balancing the "financial statements".

Responsibilities to protect the home do not stop when the sunlight dissipates over the horizon. Business affairs require extended management and the noble wife, after settling the home down for the evening rest, will make sure today's business activities will be documented in order to continue into a coming new day of responsibilities. Sometimes, more often than not, the wife and mother will sacrifice much needed rest or ensure her business affairs are not at risk due to any inattentiveness on her part.

She surrounds her home with financial responsibility in order to meet the needs of the family by the system of supply and demand. Her mind is directed to will and action over a zealous concern for her business. A profit is expected and only commitment in the retail trade will bring success. She has to be wise to thieves and crooks who may try to steal from her wealth. It could be possible she has employed an accountant and it is necessary for her to view the business affairs nightly during the peak season of harvest to market economics.

The business activities are only well-pleasing if favorable opportunities and successes are achieved. Darkness will not bring a destructible union of daytime business and its attention to details. A lamp is lit to continue the commitment of owning a business. Documentation is the key to a proper organized business. The expense of burning olive oil for light is an added cost but the rewards to see a successful business are at times expensive and necessary.

She knows meditation upon the Lord is crucial to Him blessing the business affairs but she knows her faith requires a tremendous amount of work.

There are also spiritual implications to learn in this proverb. The enemy will surround the business, and it is imperative that the spiritual fortress of the Lord has previously been established around her economic efforts. The wife can enclose the business spiritually by her relationship to the Lord. Her ownership of the business causes her to surround it with prayer by appealing to the Lord for his increase of profits. She knows meditation upon the Lord is crucial to him blessing the business affairs but she knows her faith requires a tremendous amount of work. She even continues and hopes the Lord will surround her in visionary dreams that can give her an advantage over other competitors.

"But my prayer, in righteousness, is to see your face; on waking, may I be satisfied with a vision of you" (***Psalms 17:15***).

It is easy to get caught up in a business in which that is all one meditates upon. But a noble female continues her worship of the Lord knowing a business is but a help to the family. She, as a believer, is surrounded by great cloud of witnesses (***Hebrews 12:1***) and her endurance always has trust in her Savior Yeshua for her investments. Her heart burns continuously by the Holy Spirit (***Luke 24:32***). She is a reminder to those around her of the importance of staying alert and sacrificing resting hours for a successful day in business.

Her glowing spirit will always be diligent as she abides in Yeshua ready to give a hand to any situation surrounding her financial endeavors. Her husband and children fall asleep in the flickering light of the lamp with a smile in their hearts knowing the love of a wife and mother works to embrace them with a more prosperous life.

"The crown of the wise is their riches, but the folly of fools is just that-folly." (***Proverbs 14:24***)

Let Us Reason Together

The symbolism here is very intense. When your only light flickers and finally goes out, what initial thoughts and feelings do you feel? What steps must you take to ensure that your light does not go out? In the spiritual realm, what do you accomplish by your flickering light?

What does a balanced life look like with God, family, business, community etc.?

What questions, thoughts, or feelings do you have after reading chapter nine?

NOTES

NOTES

NOTES

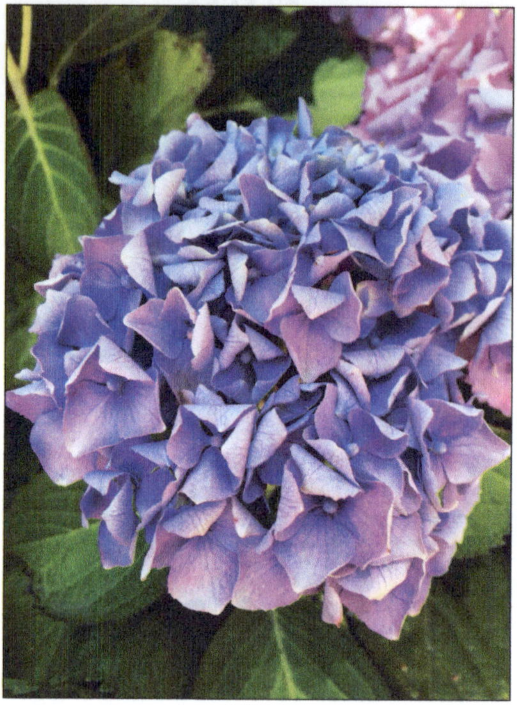

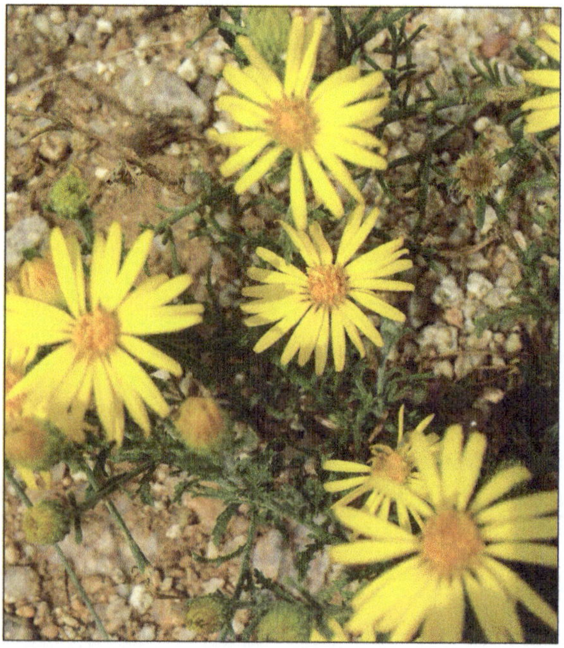

Chapter 10

SHE PUTS

"She puts her hands to the staff with the flax; her fingers hold the spinning rod." (Proverbs 31:19)

"The tenth letter of Hebrew alphabets is called "*Yod*" (rhymes with "mode") and "has the sound of "y" as in "yes."[67] Its pictorial shape depicts "a hand or closed hand"[68], or "arm and hand."[69] The symbolic meaning is "a deed or to make."[70] Another beautiful meaning is "God's hand extended to mankind."[71]

The hand is an active part of the body that performs by our consciousness and character. It can be used to sign legal deeds or used to receive property and legal rights. We all use hands to make our hearts and minds known to those around us. Females are very expressive when it comes to using their hands. The concept of "*Yod*" describes it as being mine, or it belongs to me. Putting an arm and hand close to the chest shows possession and treasure whether it's the husband, children or other loved ones. All sons, daughters, and extended family are to be valued and held close to the heart. A noble woman has made a deed in her heart by receiving those she loves with her heart's hand. Putting a loved one close to the chest reveals you are making a heartfelt deed of committed love and care. You reveal a reality of telling the loved one, you are willing to work at a right relationship.

A mother's hand is an instrument of demanded respect and used in practical ways to teach self-motivation and self-respect.

A mother can lay her hands upon a child for prayer and comfort or use her hands as a means to reveal expected respect due to a child's misbehavior. There is a Jewish proverb that says, "Parents who do not teach their children to work, train them to be thieves who covet." A mother's hand is an instrument of demanded respect and used in practical ways to teach self-motivation and self-respect.

Her arms and hands modify to get the most righteous or godly result. Hands can create only by those who have willingly learned a trade. A hand at work on God's behalf will bring Him honor and glory from the family. Even safety in the midst of turmoil, will be the result due to the activity of a female's hand (***Matthew 23: 37***). Yeshua, the Savior of the world, wanted to use his hands willingly to reach out and hold his own people, Israel. He wanted to extend his arms towards them and pull them close to his heartbeat. Those who stoned and killed the prophets of God were still loved by Yeshua. He wanted to use His hands to create a secure loving environment for His own.

A Hebrew word using "Yod" such as "ye-hu-dah"[72] is the name of the fourth son of Jacob who represented the royal tribe of Israel. A king's hand can give or take by their authority. Another Hebrew word is "yo-`el" which means "Adonai is God."[73] He was a prophet in Judah who was one of the prophets of Israel. He was a messenger to Judah who revealed God's hand of extending judgment upon His children and the nations that would invade her.

In this proverb the woman is using her hands to process flax into a usable product. If you have ever watched the process of developing flax roots into fibrous material for linen, it is an amazing task to study and watch. It requires the use of the hands and arms. This domestic operation is not an abridgment of liberty but rather a blessing and an opportunity to teach children hard work can be worth the investment of hard labor.

There is no hesitation as she flexes her arms and hands with devotion, looking to invest her time for a quality product. Her hands give, and she, along with her home, will receive the benefit and rewards of profitable labor. There is a small staff taken by the hand and used to pound on the flax root in order to break away the outer bark. Fibers began to unravel and once they are combed into a fine fibers her fingers began the process of twisting them into thread. This work demands persistence as she endures, steadfastly, the spinning of the fiber for the end product called linen. There is going to be callouses that build upon the fingers and palms, but they prove her commitment to securing further financial enterprises. The wife knows she is fulfilling God's will by assisting the husband and building care and security in the home due to her committed deed of being devoted as a wife and mother.

"Adonai will open for you His good treasure, the sky, to give your land its rain at the right seasons and to bless everything you undertake. You will lend to many nations and not borrow" (Deuteronomy 28:12).

This was a blessing spoken to Israel as a whole. The men and women using their hands in movement and action would create economic strength that would surround her people and lead the nation to be lenders. They would not be subjected to the extended hands of pagan nations if they obeyed the Lord and His Torah. Her wisdom in using her hands would strengthen the nation besides the family unit. Her hands are not going to be idle but used to embrace her loved ones or extended towards making a product to serve them well.

Following Yeshua requires our use of our hands, He has blessed us with, in order to achieve the leading of His Spirit. Serving God requires the use of one's hands. Spreading His truth that is held close to one's heart, demands focused straight forward attention. His will is to be taken serious with unwavering devotion as we extend our hands on His behalf.

"To him Yeshua said, "No one who puts his hand to the plow and keeps looking back is fit to serve in the Kingdom of God" (Luke 9:62).

<u>**Spreading His truth that is held close to one's heart, demands focused straight forward attention.**</u>

Also, the hands used to bless a family can be positioned to worship God as a means to spiritually embrace God and hold Him close to one's heart of deed and commitment. This will create a healthy spiritual relationship as He orders our footsteps day by day. In *Psalm 28:2*, we read these words,

"Hear the sound of my prayers when I cry to you, when I lift my hands toward your holy sanctuary."

As God brought Israel out of Egypt with His hand holding them close to His heart, it created a nation of freedom as an instrument to perform God's will. His hand processed their dark crusty hearts and brought out the soft pliable spirits who would finally obey Him. In the future, according to prophecy, He will gather them again with His extended hand to fulfill His ordained deed. This is done by His hand of passion.

"For I will take you from among the nations, gather you from all countries, and return you to your soil.

> *Then I will sprinkle clean water on you, and you will be clean; I will cleanse you from all your uncleanness and from all your idols. I will give you a new heart and put a new spirit inside you; I will take the stony heart out of your flesh and give you a new heart of flesh. I will put my Spirit inside you"* (*Ezekiel 36:24-27a*).

By His hand, an amazing spiritual transformation will began to take shape in Israel. They, the Jewish people, are going to experience a rebirth in Yeshua Messiah.

In going back to this proverb concerning this noble woman, we find she is extremely creative. This is a characteristic of God in human form. The Lord created the heavens with His fingers (*Psalms 8:4(3)*) and this is a definitive characteristic of a women in this proverb. She would weave a beautiful tapestry of fine linen from a bundle of hard rough flax roots. Her mother probably trained her to use her body as a testimony to her God given vision and skill. This type of spiritual fortitude and creative ability will give her an object lesson in the spiritual work of the ministry. In *1 Corinthians 9:27*, we read these words,

> *"I treat my body hard and make it my slave so that, after proclaiming the Good News to others, I myself will not be disqualified."*

A noble woman's efforts in the spiritual realm are second to no one as she grasps the Torah in spirit, mind, and body. These qualities will prove to be useful to the destitute and poor outside of the family home.

"You will be a glorious crown in the hand of Adonai, a royal diadem held by your God." (Isaiah 62:3)

Let Us Reason Together

What are your hands busy doing?

Describe the passion in your hands. Do you have a passion that uses your hands to reach out to others?

Take a moment and look at your hands. Are you satisfied with them? What would you like your hands to look like? To be doing?

What questions, thoughts, or feelings do you have after reading chapter ten?

NOTES

NOTES

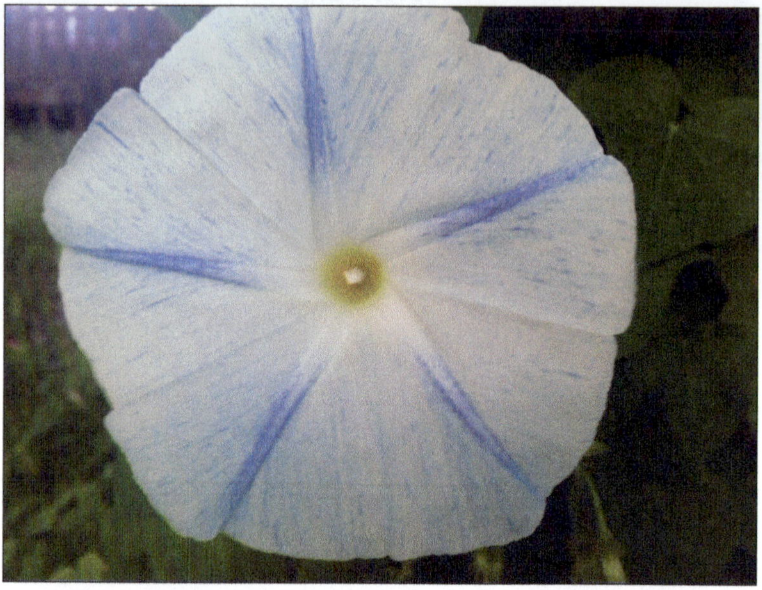

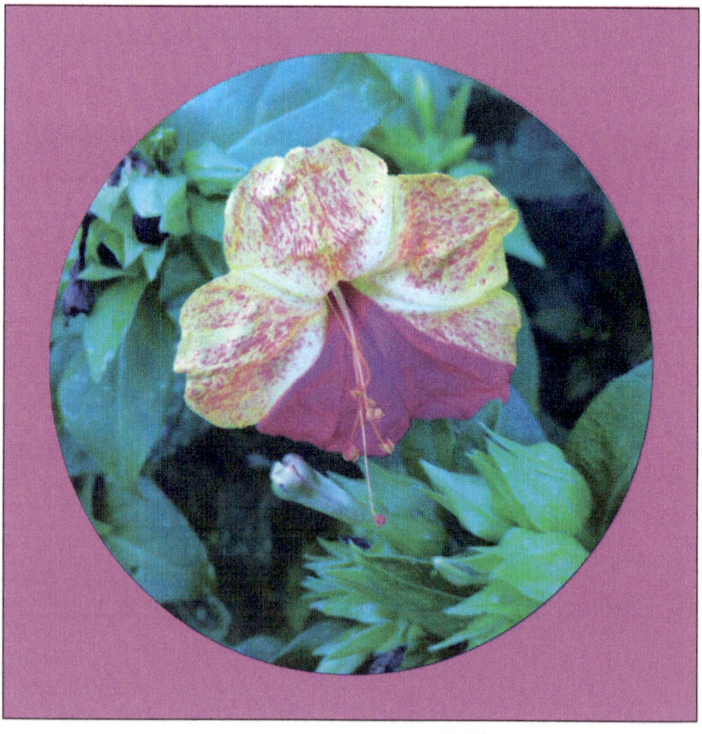

Chapter 11

SHE REACHES

"She reaches out to embrace the poor and opens her arms to the needy." (Proverbs 31:20)

The eleventh letter of the Hebrew alphabet is called "*Kaf*" and has the sound of "k" as in "kangaroo".[74] The paleo-Hebrew shape represents "an arm, or open hand."[75] It can also mean "palm of a hand."[76] Symbolically it means to "cover, allow."[77] It can also convey the reality of God "holding us in the "hollow" of His hand, the hand bruised for us."[78]

My personal experiences in life knows the gift of a female's open-armed embrace. Someone to really care when one is in desperate need of deliverance. There are times in life when you need a righteous woman to love and encourage you with God's love and protection. I have experienced the loving arms of a female to reach out with Christ's love and it is priceless! Also, there is a concept of using one's arm to extend an open hand to cover the mouth of accusers or those who use hurtful words against the sinner. Historically and biblically speaking, the poor and needy were considered the worst of sinners living a life well deserved for their sin. People spoke harshly and accused the poor. We find accusers of this sort in the book of Job. Man's religion at its finest hour! Thank the Lord Yeshua Messiah who reached out His arm and embraced me, the worst of sinners.

A Hebrew word using the letter "Kaf" well known among Bible scholars is "ko-hen ga-dol" which means High Priest.[79] Ultimately this individual is responsible to ensure the poor and needy are being taken care of by the tithes of Israel. His arms and open hands are the earthly instruments he uses to embrace those in need. This is an act of worship to God. He is to use his arms and hands to direct the Levites, the priestly tribe, to embrace the poor and needy as God directs him.

Another beautiful Hebrew word is "ke-tav haq-qo-desh" which means "Holy writings; Scriptures."[80] The arm and hand grasp the writing utensil used to bring glory to God and blessings to people. God reached out through men to write His truth to mankind by written revelation using the DNA of creation which is the Hebrew alphabet. It is an amazing journey into learning how scribes write the Torah Scripture with great passion letter by letter. I have read that there are close to six thousand rules to follow when hand writing the Torah.

A noble wife is a woman of grace and forgiveness who stops the mouths of those who judge others.

Likewise a noble woman reaches out to embrace the poor with passion and compassion. "No woman would be complete unless she had a social conscience."[81] If one's heart is quick to speak harsh words against another then she would use her hand to cover their mouths. A noble wife is a women of grace and forgiveness who stops the mouths of those who judge others. She reaches out to the poor and needy to bring love, restoration and a sense of godly worth to the individual in need.

In this proverb, the righteous woman is used by the Lord to freely give to the poor and those who are in need. As she walks through the city streets she takes notice of the destitute and due to her financial abundance, she is able to take decisive effective action. ***Psalms 112:9*** tells us,

> ***"He distributes freely, he gives to the poor; his righteousness stands forever."***

The character of nobility provides for the poor with shared financial liberality. This is not about a slothful rich female who garners attention through giving, but rather a prudent woman who diligently works hard and is, "intent on giving as well as getting."[82] Therefore, in this rational approach of enlarging her care beyond the home she welcomes, feeds and nurtures those with true needs. Her knowledge and heartfelt compassion puts her arms and hands to task.

There are numerous reasons for poverty among society. Greed, covetousness, laziness, prejudices and faithlessness toward God are a few of many reasons for causing men, women, and children to hunger spiritually, emotionally and physically. A woman of such valor seeks to find and understand each situation of the poor while at the same time develops a plan of action to relieve hunger and want.

"The righteous understands the cause of the poor, but the wicked is unconcerned" (Proverbs 29:7).

The Proverbs 31 woman shamelessly reaches out with a broken heart to the beggars and despised of society.

The *Proverbs 31* woman shamelessly reaches out with a broken heart to the beggars and despised of society. Whether widows, orphans, or strangers she finds that extended "family" in society and shows her liberality by giving food, clothing and comfort. Due to man's sin and rebellion the world has unfolded into corruption. One aspect of corruption is the poverty of man which effects the whole of society. She is going to alleviate the situation as best she can with her financial capability.

Yeshua the Messiah said *"You always have the poor among you, but you will not always have me" (John 12:8).* In this context He was talking about His impending death while some were grumbling about a blessing of worship poured out upon him by a woman. True even though the poor are among us it is proper to bless the Lord financially with our offerings. But the fact is, poverty exists and the arms of compassion must act accordingly in loving embrace.

> *"Always treat others as you would like them to treat you; that sums up the teachings, of the Torah and the Prophets." (Matthew 7:12)*

The noble wife is a testimony to this truth. Her arms are filled with abundance and she willfully supplements, by her wealth, the necessities of helping the poor even during lean times in her home. What a great testimony of a noble wife! One who is rich spiritually in the Lord, she also gives from her blessings of financial abundance. This is a fruit of righteousness that comes from and through such a woman.

> *"Moreover, God has the power to provide you with every gracious gift in abundance, so that always in every way you will have all you need yourselves and be able to provide abundantly for every good cause" (2 Corinthians 9:8).*

"Filled with the fruit of righteousness that comes through Yeshua the Messiah- to the glory and praise of God" (Philippians 1:11).

She is but a willing vessel to enthusiastically embrace the destitute. To wrong the poor is to despise the Creator. Yeshua is not only Savior but He is Supreme over all things (***Colossians 1:15-17***). Not only does He watch and work through a willing vessel but her husband see's the arm and hand of God working in and through her. She counters those who oppress the poor and serve the rich. We read these words in ***Proverbs 22:16***,

"Both oppressing the poor to enrich oneself and giving to the rich yield only loss."

A husband of such a woman who fights poverty and oppression is blessed and honored. The temptation to only befriend the wealthy, for social status and honor, has no place in a noble woman's heart. She fights against poverty and want. She knows to empathize with the broken-hearted and the down and out. Due to her giving, the Lord blesses the home and she has no fear of want and need. This is a covenantal promise God made to compassionate givers.

"Cherish her, and she will exalt you; embrace her, and she will bring you honor; and she will give your

*head a garland of grace, bestow on you a crown of glory." (**Proverbs 4:8-9**)*

Let Us Reason Together

When you see someone standing at the corner begging for food or a job, what are your first thoughts? Why? Who taught you to think like that?

How do you think the ***Proverbs 31*** woman would respond in her heart? If Yeshua were to give you divine appointments today, helping others meet their basic needs, how would you respond?

What questions, thoughts, or feelings do you have after reading chapter eleven?

NOTES

NOTES

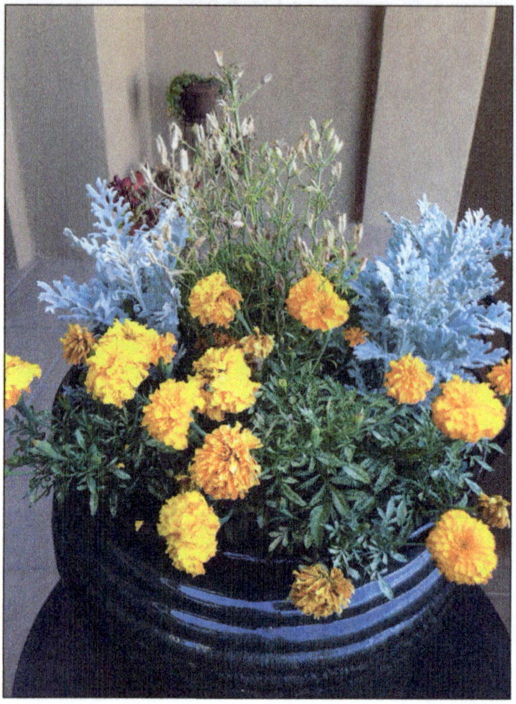

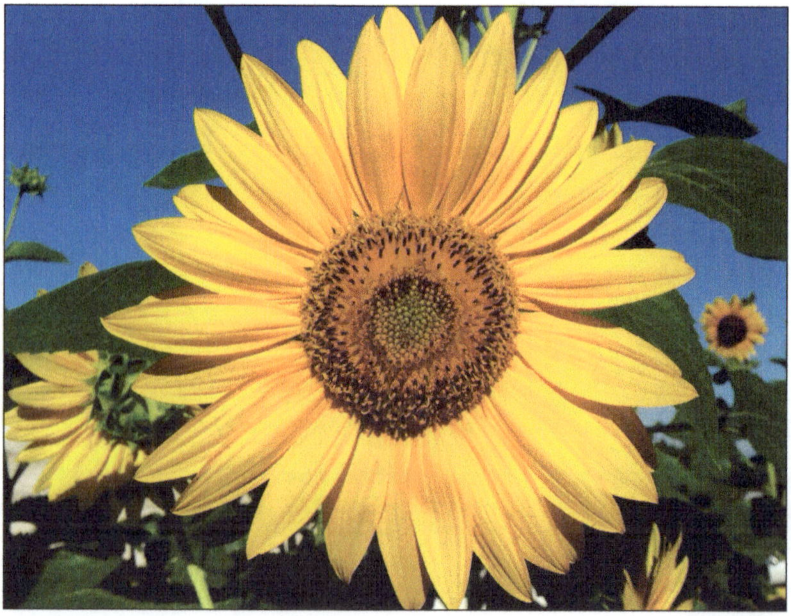

Chapter 12

WHEN IT SNOWS

"When it snows, she has no fear for her household; since all of them are doubly clothed." (Proverbs 31:21)

"The twelfth letter of the Hebrew alphabet is called "Lamed" (pronounced "lah-med") and has the sound of "l" as in "love."[83] Its pictographic shape is a "cattle goad or a staff."[84] Another pictorial representation is "a yoke."[85] The symbolic meaning is "prod, toward,"[86] or control,[87] as with a yoke upon an ox. "Lamed" represents the first controller or one who is in authority or control over the situation. The staff can prod a person toward the pathway to righteous living. The controller's wisdom in the Torah is a yoke or staff that controls their will to make righteous decisions according to God's plan and purpose.

There are two beautiful Hebrew words that use the letter "Lamed." The first is "le-viy-yim" which means "Levites."[88] This is the tribe that brought religious authority over Israel. They were the controllers on how to worship God. In unusual situations, the High Priest inquired the Lord Yehovah for answers and by his authority he, the High Priest, executed the Lords answer accordingly. The second word is "le-chem", which means "bread."[89] Yeshua is the Bread of Life. He is our eternal Savior who holds the rod of iron and rules as a true Shepherd. A true shepherd feeds his sheep and takes care of them when the cold weather approaches. By his or her staff, they will lead them and take control over the situation to the best of their ability.

The Lord said He created times and seasons, and the wife will prepare for the coming weather accordingly. In this proverb, snow represents the unusual. As the six-pointed ice crystals, shaped like the Star of David, fall to the ground, the wise woman is already prepared to take care of her household. Cold weather can bring apprehension and anxiety if one is not prepped. But due to her mastery over the home she is ready to protect those living inside the home as they must walk to the Synagogue or the market.

The double clothing is but an extension of herself. As the husband walks to the city gates or the children attend school, their warmth is but a reminder of the one who loves and cares for them. A noble wife who loves and cares for her family is ever on their minds. She is revealed as a confident and prepared leader in the home. One who holds the staff takes control of the situation or circumstances with a foresight for the future.

Not to be confused with worry, she is knowledgeable concerning weather patterns. She has prepared beforehand for the cold and has made doubly sure her family will be adequately taken care of for even colder weather. A noble wife doesn't show unhealthy concern or worry about her husband and children in dangerous weather conditions. She has lived through enough seasons and years knowing the cycles of weather patterns can be reasonably estimated but sometimes unpredictable. In these Bible times weather forecasting was extremely limited to the surrounding visible horizon. But she has no fear because the household has been prodded in the spring and summer months to harvest and prepare for the coming cold season. She has made enough linen to dress her family warmly for the winter weather.

Some biblical translations from Hebrew to English use the words "shonim" or "shenayim" which means "scarlet" or "double thickness respectively.[90] This could mean a sign of luxury or one well prepared in excess. In the whole context of the **Proverbs 31** woman, in my view, both interpretations have merit. God has blessed this noble woman with abundance and intelligence.

It is easy to see the wealthy dress for the cold as compared to the poor. This proverb reminds me of the book collection "Little House on the Prairie" series. Laura Ingalls Wilder writes about her husband growing up on a farm in eastern United States. In the book titled "*Farmer Boy*", we discover his mother is a woman who exemplifies this proverb. Almanzo's mother is an excellent example of a well prepared woman ready for the cold season.

We, as humans, are to trust those who protect us from the unpredictable elements. These domestic traits of preparing beforehand have a spiritual source. Her potential fear of being unprepared will reflect a flawed character about her spiritual nobility. But her righteousness and love of God will manifest towards her family in the daily and seasonal needs of life. She is not going to allow her family to reflect her failure to prepare for the coming cold season. They are going to be well dressed for the season.

By her wisdom, a wise female will prepare well for the home.

One who fears the Lord will learn His way and wisdom. God has ordained seasons, months, and years (***Ecclesiastes 3:1-8***). By her wisdom a wise female will prepare well for the home. ***Proverbs 9:1-6*** tells us,

> *"Wisdom has built herself a house; she has carved her seven pillars. She has prepared her food, spiced her wine, and she has set her table. She has sent out her young girls (with invitations); she calls from the heights of the city, "Whoever is unsure of himself, turn in here!" To someone weak-willed she says, "Come and eat my food! Drink the wine I have mixed! Don't stay unsure of yourself, but live! Walk in the way of understanding!"*

Wisdom's house is built with seven pillars which refers to the Creation story. God has given mankind six days to work and prepare accordingly prior to the day of rest, Shabbat. Her character is likened to one of the pillars of a home. She has taken authority over the situation and a sense of security is felt by the husband and children. To her it would be "utter folly"[91] to send out her family unprepared into the cold. She would be judged by God and her treatment of her husband and children is an accountability she takes serious.

Her children are the future of Israel and they will be taken care of under her staff and yoke. The wisdom of a noble woman is used while she looks into the, not so distant future. Her lack of fear has counteracted folly and unprepared foolish behavior.[92] Her name is worn all over her husband and children as they display, doubly, a wife and mother who has planned accordingly.

Her name is worn all over her husband and children as they display, doubly, a wife and mother who has planned accordingly.

> *"Idle hands bring poverty; diligent hands bring wealth. A sensible person gathers in the summer, be he who sleeps during harvest is an embarrassment" (Proverbs 10:4-5).*

She has no fear of having the reputation of being an idle and unprepared woman. Even in the New Covenant Scriptures, the Apostle Sha'ul (Paul) instructs Timothy to instruct the women to take charge of their homes (***1 Timothy 5:14***). In addition, a woman who does not provide for her family is called something worse than an unbeliever (***1 Timothy 5:8***).

The home desperately needs the noble female to take control of unusual situations. Her spiritual hunger and worship towards the Lord will ensure provision for the home (***1 Kings 8:37-40***). Her use of the staff and yoke in the home, with humility, will ensure the blessing of God's prosperity. The words of ***1 Peter 5:6*** make this fairly clear,

> *"Therefore, humble yourself under the mighty hand of God, so that at the right time he may lift you up. Throw all you anxieties upon him, because he cares about you."*

In turn, this will protect chaos from forming in the home and will bring joy and life to the family. Children who are cared for are a reflection of the home's leadership. People can look at the children on a cold wintery day and judge whether the mother does or does not care for her prodigy.

Our Savior is the perfect representation of the letter "Lamed". He demonstrates this reality in ***Psalms 23***. He is our Shepherd who will ensure His sheep lack nothing and are well fed. We rest in knowing He controls our situation and guides into right paths. Disasters or cold weather will come but we, as His children, will not fear because His staff reassures us. Every day of our lives will have grace and goodness as the years pass. A noble female is a reflection of this Psalm.

"Then, when the Chief Shepherd appears, you will receive glory as your unfading crown." (1 Peter 5:4)

Let Us Reason Together

We all know someone who never seems to be prepared for anything. They borrow things without returning them. They wait until the last minute to begin projects. When you see that person coming in your direction, what are your initial thoughts?

Perhaps you are that person. What steps do you need to take to begin planning ahead?

How can a procrastinator become a prepared person who blesses others in a timely manner?

What questions, thoughts, or feelings do you have after reading chapter twelve?

NOTES

NOTES

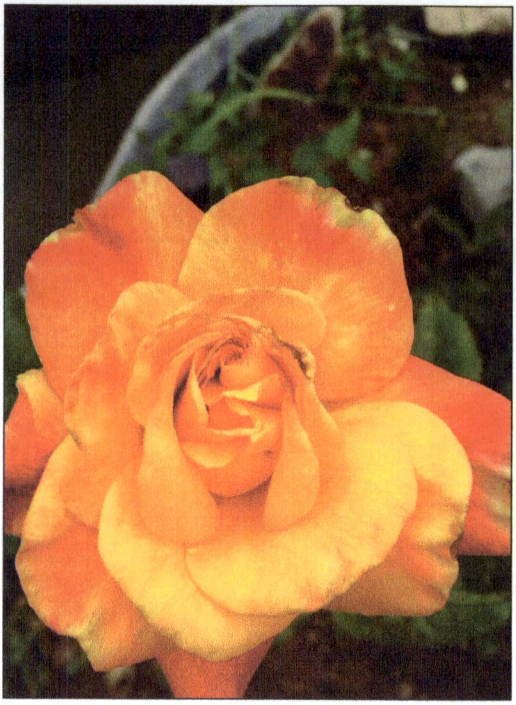

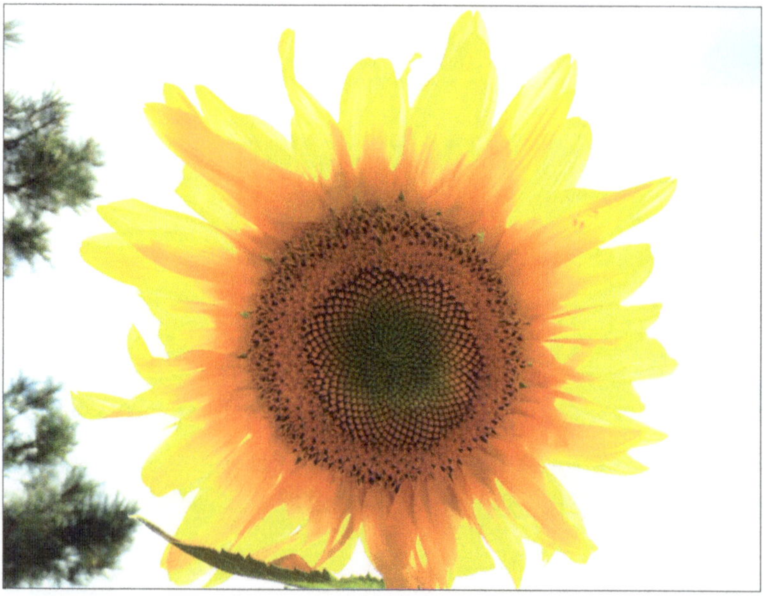

Chapter 13

SHE MAKES

"She makes her own quilts; she is clothed in fine linen and purple."(Proverbs 31:22)

The thirteenth letter of the Hebrew alphabet is called "Mem" and has the sound of "m" as in "mother".[93] Its Paleo-Hebrew shape represents "water"[94] or "waves of the sea."[95] The symbolic meaning is "chaos or massive."[96] In this context of this particular proverb, "water" and "massive" are the key meanings to this teaching. Conceptually water represents the life of a mother always there, always faithful. It's a biblical prophecy that Havah (Eve) was gifted to bring the light of Life into the world. The faithfulness of a female is life to those around her. She can be used by the Lord to bring refreshing life into the direst of circumstances.

There are so many examples in Scripture of women bringing life back to the nation of Israel's communities and homes. The book of Ruth and Samuel reveal women who brought "water" back to the nation of Israel. They were Ruth and Hannah respectively. In spite of difficult circumstances, their faith in the Lord carried them through chaos and their "massive water" of spirit brought life, in God's unique way through them, back into the Israelite tribes. After Ruth vowed to connect with the Jewish people she was redeemed by Boaz and her offspring became the royal line of Israel. Hannah dedicated her son Samuel to the Lord and through this prophet, David was anointed to be king over Israel.

Several Hebrew words using the letter "Mem" relate to the idea of water, and life. One is called "mab-bul" which means flood.[97] God brought a massive flood of water to destroy the wickedness of man in order to bring spiritual life back to mankind through Noah. Another Hebrew word is "mid-rash" which means exegesis, interpretation or investigation.[98] Anyone who applies these principles, by the leading of the Holy Spirit, to Scripture will gain the Living Water of Life; spiritually, emotionally and physically. Of course the all-important word using "Mem" is "mo-shi-a'" which means Savior.[99] Yeshua the Moshia destroyed our spiritual chaos and massively brought believers in Him the living moving water of salvation.

> *"Yeshua, answered, "Everyone who drinks this water will get thirsty again, but whoever drinks the water I will give him will never be thirsty again! On the contrary, the water I give him will become a spring of water inside him, welling up into eternal life"* (***John 4:13-14***)!

In this proverb, I believe the female reader is going to be blessed by this exegesis of Scripture. This particular proverb was difficult to explain on how to relate water and life in connection with her making quilts and being clothed in fine linen and purple. But it is easier than one might think. We so far have read about the testimony of a noble wife in previous proverbs. She is a very busy woman, spiritually, emotionally, mentally, and physically.

You cannot give life if you are not full of life.

A woman, gifted by the Lord, is a creator, one who prepares and one of splendid royalty. In order to create true life of blessings in the home, she has to possess a sense of self-esteem and exceptional quality. You cannot give life if you are not full of life. This proverb reveals how such a wife expresses her femininity and artistic abilities.

The translation that she "makes her own quilts" is questionable. This woman, through careful creative activity is making fine designer clothing for herself and home decor. Elegant wear, cushions, tapestry and bed coverings all play into her life as a sensual woman as well as a mother and employer. She is not just a wife and mother but rather at times a woman that is sexually passionate with her husband. The book *Song of Songs* explains it well. It is a romantic story of a lovers who are extremely passionate about each other. Through some trials and tribulation their spiritual, emotional and sexual passion never fails. It is biblical proof the Lord wants a man and woman to enjoy the romantic pleasures of life. Even in the midst of a busy life of raising a family, the lovers are to allow time for passionate love.

A noble wife will make time for herself away from the domestic and business affairs of life. She wants to clothe herself in the best of linen clothing and makeup. Her home is full of self-created tapestries hanging within the home. Nice furniture and beautiful stylish clothing brings the beauty out of a woman who wants to express herself in confidence and elegance.

This fine linen is of purple and white. These are colors of victory, purity and joy. Every woman wants to look and feel good about herself. It is imperative, she does not neglect her needs and expressive designs. Her character of a godly spirit will be displayed in her home décor but especially her clothing and physical appearance. She wants to look and feel her best and it is important she gives herself times of self-refreshment. If she fails in this area she is but a slave to her family. A quiet hot scented bath, a flickering candle and a glass of wine can do wonders for a woman. Trust me, I know.

The spiritual reality of this proverb is beautiful. *Isaiah 61:10* tell us,

> *"I am so joyful in Adonai! My soul rejoices in my God, for he has clothed me in salvation, dressed me with a robe of triumph, like a bridegroom wearing a festive turban, like a bride adorned with her jewels."*

How can God adorn with salvation and triumph if He Himself is not Salvation and Triumph? So too, a noble wife has to give herself time in God's Word away from the affairs of life in order to keep the life giving frame of mind to bring life ("water") and joy to the family. She has prepared for herself, to have that good appearance and self-refreshment that would help lead her to an exceptional display of a godly life with refreshing joy.

> *"Let us rejoice and be glad! Let us give him the glory! For the time has come for the wedding of the Lamb, and his Bride has prepared herself-fine linen, bright and clean has been given her to wear" (Revelation 19:7-8).*

<u>*Ultimately it is not the expensive clothing or luxurious living but rather the life giving love that is portrayed at the city gates.*</u>

Ultimately it is not the expensive clothing or luxurious living (*Luke 16:19*) but rather the life giving love that is portrayed at the city gates. Times of personal reflection and refreshment are necessary in order to be a woman who can bring active life-giving water to those around her.

> *"I gave you jewelry to wear, bracelets for your hands, a necklace for your neck, a ring for your nose,*

earrings for your ears and a beautiful crown for your head." (Ezekiel 16:11-12)

Let Us Reason Together

What *life* can you bring into the lives of those around you?

Upon what do you base your own self-esteem? Is it your faith, what others say about you or how you feel about yourself?

When you take time away from the routines of daily life, how do you feel? Husbands, what are your thoughts when your wife asks for some alone time?

What questions, thoughts, or feelings do you have after reading chapter thirteen?

NOTES

NOTES

NOTES

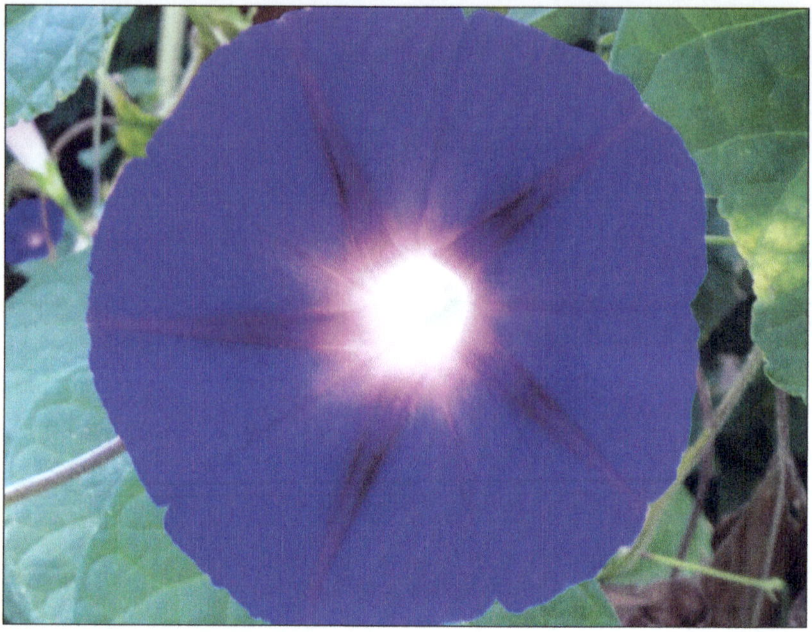

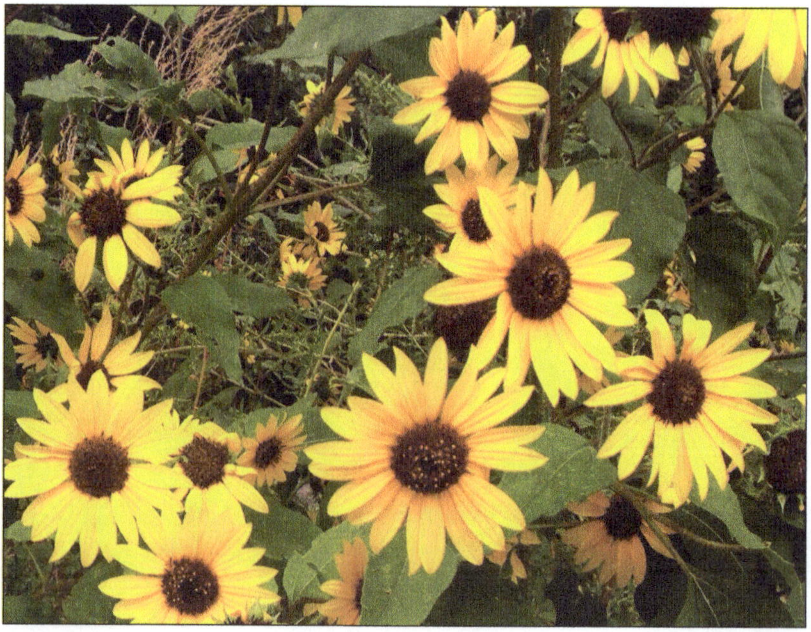

Chapter 14

HER HUSBAND IS KNOWN

"Her husband is known at the city gates when he sits with the leaders of the land." (Proverbs 31:23)

"The fourteenth letter of the Hebrew alphabet is called "Nun" (pronounced "noon").[100] It carries the sound of "n" as in "not".[101] Its pictorial shape means "fish moving",[102] or "seed."[103] The symbolic meaning is "activity or life."[104] Fish are constantly moving in and through active water. They live an active life and are very quick. The concept really points heavily toward action or life given through a person spiritually, emotionally and physically. Its life force, so to speak, in all things like the God kind of life. Human life after Adam and Eve started with a seed and turned into a viable moving human being with a spirit, soul and body. The seed is the smallest part of organic development and it eventually germinates into one of its own kind.

Life is the spiritual or physical vitality that characterizes all of humanity. Life brings a host of action and liveliness. For example, the Hebrew word "dan" is a combination of two letters "Dalet" and "Nun". These two letters represent door and life respectively. "Dan" translates from Hebrew to English as meaning judge. A judge can bring life or death to a person. They can give mercy and redemption to one who deserves death. A judge's decision can be a door to life. Yeshua took on our judgment of deserved death and gave us a new life in Him.

> *"I am the gate; if someone enters through me, he will be safe and will go in and out and find pasture. The thief comes only in order to steal, kill, and destroy; I have come so that they may have life, life in its fullest measure" (John 10:9-10).*

A Hebrew word using the Hebrew letter "Nun" is "ne-chush-tan" which translates to "The Brass Serpent".[105] Those Israelites who were bitten by the snakes in the wilderness wanderings could look up at the brass serpent and live to see another day on earth.

> *"...Moshe prayed for the people, and Adonai answered Moshe: "Make a poisonous snake and put it on a pole. When anyone who has been bitten sees it, he will live" (Numbers 21:7b-8).*

The last example is "ne-vi-'im" which means prophets.[106] All the prophets of God used words to bring destruction or life to Israel.

Many times the prophets of the Lord gave the Israelites hope in dire circumstances. God's spoken Word, through the prophets, can give life back to the spiritual and physical makeup of a nation.

In this proverb, the city gate is the backdrop to this extension of a noble woman. The city gates are known as an area of activity and life. Merchants selling food, clothing, jewelry, spices and a host of other wares line the entrances inside and outside of the gates pathways. Even the King of Israel, at times, would sit by the city gates and judge the people. Today in Israel, the city gates in Jerusalem are extremely exciting when entering or exiting. So much activity among people coming and going through the gates of the Crown Jewel of the World, Jerusalem. The capital of Israel and the world.

A reputation as a wise and respected man of the Lord can result from being blessed with a spiritually beautiful woman as a wife of noble character.

The noble woman has a husband who is honorable and dignified as he along with other elders arrive and sit at the gates for religious or political reasons. He is well known at the city gates and one of the reasons is the fact he is married to a godly wise woman. A reputation as a wise and respected man of the Lord can result from being blessed with a spiritually beautiful woman as a wife of noble character. It would be highly likely this husband is one of noble character himself. Chances are, the parents of such a woman would only give their daughter to a man of God-fearing character worthy of their daughter. The husband through the extended arm and hands of such a wife, will also be honorable due to the righteous management of the children. Even his children bring him a life-giving respectable name. This is also the result of a noble wife who has trained her children to fear the Lord.

No one wants to be judged by a man whose wife is of ill repute or whose children are ungodly. This wife is going to make sure her family are life givers to themselves and the community. Part of a man managing his family is done by the wife as his co-equal in marriage. Her voice and authority is his voice and authority. Her reputation among society is his reputation among society. Especially the elders of the community. We read these words in *1 Timothy 3:4*,

> *"He must manage his own household well, having children who obey him with all proper respect;"*

The quality of an elder at the city gate has an inner orientation of a moral righteous attitude. His household was established under the watchful care of a guarded female. Her character is displayed in and through her husband's prominence at a place of high visibility and movement. There is discussion of approval or disapproval among the elders concerning the Torah's ruling. Their rulings and interpretations can give or take life from anyone in the local community. This particular husband's understanding of the Torah is highly respected.

Her Husband Is Known

Her husband's conduct of truth, righteousness and virtue (***Philippians 4:8***) are the reflections of his wife. The husband sits among the leaders as a mark of distinction. This official life among the inhabitants of Israel relies in the spiritual strength of the elders. Fortunately this husband is blessed and he knows his home is managed well by the wife. This enables him to focus and give time to helping the community to live orderly lives under God's Torah. I'm confident he even confides in her for help to make righteous and timely decisions at the city gates. She is a productive life-giving co-equal to her husband.

People talk about each other. They slander, gossip or speak ill of individuals constantly. The city gates were no exception to the rule in Israel. Even the New Covenant Church had these sinful issues. But when this husband is spoken of, his name brings endearing words of respect and love among his peers.

Yeshua Messiah sits with the Elder of all elders; namely His Father. Through God the Holy Spirit, He continually gives life or takes life from his enemies. His place of authority reveals an eternal judge of perfect reputation and is known worldwide at all city gates. I have been to the city gates of Jerusalem. Walking through the city gates and the walls ramparts His name was spoken of constantly. Today Yeshua sits next to His Father in heaven ready and prepared to finish His Father's business.

> *"Adonai says to my Lord, "Sit at my right hand, until I make your enemies you footstool" (Psalms 110:1).*

Yeshua Messiah rules with His powerful scepter. He is led of the Holy Spirit in perfect fullness expecting His future Bride to bring Him honor and respect as she should. The Church is the supporter of her future husband, Yeshua, and her reputation is a factor on how people act towards or speak about His name at the city gates. The Body of Christ is the biggest supporter of Yeshua our Savior and Lover.

> *"His enemies I will clothe with shame, but on him there will be a shining crown." (Psalms 132:18)*

Let Us Reason Together

Where are most of your family decisions made?
Who makes important family decisions?
How would you rate your leadership skills? Those of your spouse?
What steps do you need to take to be an encouragement to each other and develop a stronger team approach to problem solving?

What questions, thoughts, or feelings do you have after reading chapter fourteen?

NOTES

NOTES

NOTES

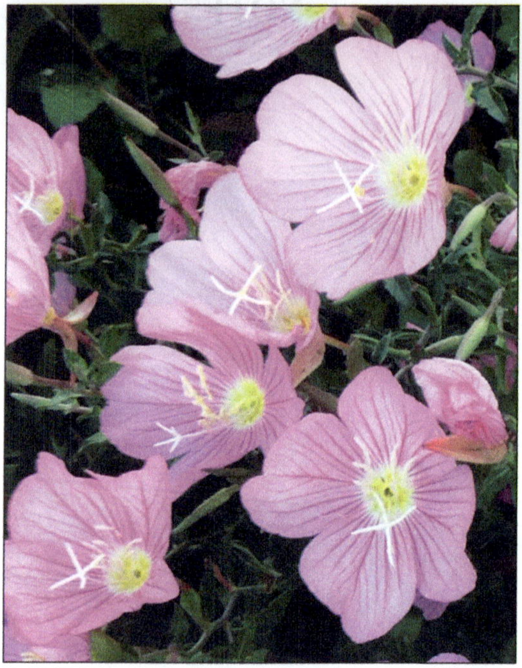

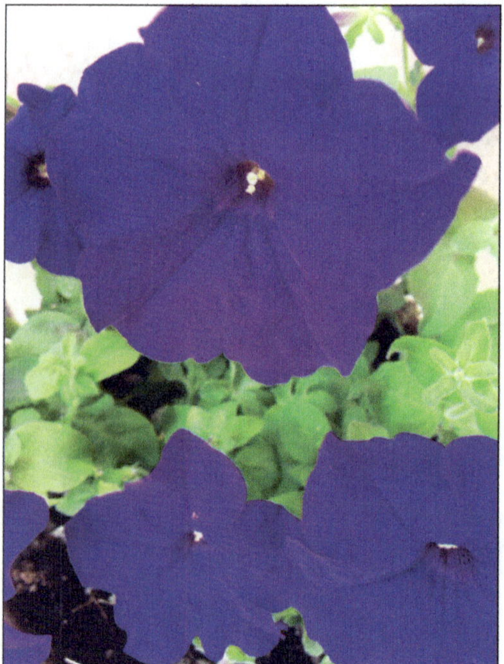

Chapter 15

SHE MAKES LINEN GARMENTS

"She makes linen garments and sells them; she supplies the merchants with sashes." (Proverbs 31:24)

"The fifteenth letter of the Hebrew alphabet is called "Samekh" (pronounced "sah-mekh") and has the sound of "s" as in "sing".[107] The pictorial shape is a staff,[108] or a "prop."[109] The symbolic meaning is "to support"[110], "turn"[111], or "rest."[112] The concept is an object used to support a tent or a fence. A secure fence or wall around a home can be shored up by the use of a prop. It helps to secure and hold an object in place as needed. Ropes and large pins hammered into the ground were used to prop up and support the "Tent of Meeting" and the surrounding linen fence (***Exodus 27:19***).

One of my favorite words that contains the Hebrew letter "Samekh" is "sid-rah"[113] which describes the portion of the Torah that is read at the synagogue each Shabbat until the entire Torah is read each Jewish calendar year. The first five books of the Bible are divided up into "sections" and read out loud as a support to the worship service. This secures the spiritual knowledge into the minds and hearts of the hearers. Salvation can come to those who hear the Word of God. We need God's Word to support or prop our spiritually rich journey in Yeshua Messiah.

After all, the Torah points to and speaks about Yeshua Messiah who in types and shadows is the greater One to come and save the world. His truth should cause men to turn to Him for spiritual life. Yeshua is our support and prop for rest. The Bible says He is our Shabbat rest. Rest each week supports our weary bodies from a hard work week as well as our spirits and minds.

"So there remains a Shabbat-keeping for God's people. For the one who has entered God's rest has also rested from his own works, as God did from his" (Hebrews 4:9).

Another Hebrew word using "Samekh" is "suk-kah."[114] This is a temporary hut or tent built next to a home during the Feast of Tabernacles called "Sukkot". A celebration all believers in Yeshua should honor. This hut is propped up and supported with branches and fruit decorations to memorialize the wilderness wonderings in tents as their places of habitation. It gave them a thankful remembrance of eventually entering the Promised Land and having the blessing of agriculture and cities in their own covenantal homeland. National homeland stability, with the capital of Jerusalem propped up the Jewish nation in the land of Israel. It secured their identity culturally and built financial prosperity. Most of all, they had inherited land that gave them a sense of ownership and pride.

Another well-known word in Hebrew is "san-hed-rin"[115] which was the high court of judicial-executive Torah laws in the land of Israel. Civil and religious laws were debated and announced judiciously upon just about any given circumstance. This court can prop up or reinforces the stability of society whether religious or civil. Israel was a religio-political nation in which there was no separation of religion and state.

Her efforts supported or propped the financial strength of the home.

In this proverb, the woman is recognized as a prop or support to her husband by the use of her wise activity in the business of trading and selling. The Mediterranean coast of Israel is host to the mercantile business of worldwide revenue. Thousands of ships coming and going with seafarers and entrepreneurs gives a woman an opportunity to make and trade with fine linen. Her industrious spirit brought an expression in the business of profit and investment.[116] Her efforts supported and propped the financial strength of the home.

The interpretation of this proverb could be garments of brilliant white flax. Her artisan quality displayed her creative ability to attract the potential buyer due to her exceptional skill to weave a finer stronger material used for sashes and belts. In order for her to prop and support the expenses of running a home, she understands the industry needs of supply and demand. Weaving linen was hard tedious work and the knowledge of making the rightful uses of the flax was very important. The weather patterns gave maritime a small window of opportunity to move about the sea. She had to have her inventory ready to go.

Her garments are beautiful tapestry of artisan expression but it's the sashes that supplement the success of her trade. Sashes need to be strong to support the garments worn. These sashes are used to gird as a belt. Her products are esteemed highly by those who want to stock their inventory. She sees the value in her work and in turn becomes an important partner in supporting the home and interacting religiously with outsiders.

Providing a commodity of a high quality opens the doors to a healthy successful business.

Providing a commodity of a high quality opens the doors to a healthy successful business. In turn it provides a foundation of financial strength that helps to secure the financial stability of the home. Then the husband can achieve his best for the Lord by having the time to study the Torah and perform the civil duties at the city gates. Financial wealth should lead to more time given for Scripture study instead of excessive recreation or the development of worthless time-stealing hobbies.

There is a very real spiritual aspect of a woman who engages in honest high quality trade. Her interactions with the merchants provides opportunity to the sharing of God's love and salvation. Those who abide in honest business practices have a better opportunity to reach the lost for Yeshua Messiah.

Priscilla and Aquila (*Acts 18:26*) were a married Jewish couple who wove tent material and were believers in Yeshua Messiah. They worked together in the mercantile business and accompanied the apostle Paul and helped spread the Gospel. Their creative skills enabled them to travel and financially prop their affairs in the Gospel of Christ.

> *"Yeshua came and talked with them. He said, "All authority in heaven and on earth has been given to me. Therefore, go and make people from all nations into talmidim, immersing them into the reality of the Father, the Son and the Ruach HaKodesh" (Matthew 28:18-19).*

It takes material finances for such a wonderful purpose in life. Ultimately business ventures lead to the giving of God's tithe and our offerings. Not only do her efforts prop the financial strength of the home but it supports her husband as he works hard to prosper the home. Her eyes see the financial as well as the spiritual implications of a prosperous home. A woman's place is not in the home. That is a false teaching perpetrated by cultural philosophy. These proverbs prove my point. There are domestic responsibilities, but I believe the woman should always seek an opportunity to get outside of the house and use her business skills to "prop" the needs of the home and use her heart to interact with those around her spiritually.

> *"No one who has kindled a lamp hides it or places it under a bowl; rather, he puts it on a stand, so that those coming in may see its light"* (*Luke 11:33*).

> *"On that day Adonai their God will save them as the flock of his people; for they will be like gems in a crown, sparkling over his countryside."* Zechariah 9:16

Let Us Reason Together

When was the last time you have had the opportunity to share Jesus with a business associate?

How did you respond in the moment?

What did you share?

What prevents you from talking about Jesus and all the great things He has done for you?

What questions, thoughts, or feelings do you have after reading chapter fifteen?

NOTES

NOTES

NOTES

NOTES

Chapter 16

CLOTHED WITH STRENGTH

"Clothed with strength and dignity, she can laugh at the days to come." (Proverbs 31:25)

"The sixteenth letter of the Hebrew alphabet called "Ayin" (pronounced "ah-yeen")."[117] It has no sound but carries the vowel associated with it, in Scripture.[118] Its pictographic shape means an "eye",[119] or "a mouth of a spring."[120] The symbolic meaning is "to see, or to know."[121] It could also mean "a source or never ending supply."[122]

These descriptions fit a female well. Women use their eyes to constantly watch their surrounding and usually pickup on the hardest to notice attitudes and social cues of those around them. Women, in my view, seem to see spiritually with the gift of discernment and listen to the Holy Spirit with a word of knowledge more than men. This has been my experience among the Body of Christ.

Hebrew words using the letter "Ayin" such as "`a-vo-dah" means work, labor and worship; specifically in the worship duties of the sacrificial Temple services by the Great High Priest.[123] If anyone had an eye on things and had to know the Torah thoroughly, it was the High Priest. He had to keep rightful order in God's Tent because he had to enter the Holy of Holies on behalf of himself and the nation of Israel. A watchful eye on the proper activity of worship toward God meant life or death to himself or Israel. One disrespectful violation of the Torah meant sudden death or a curse by God.

Another word using "Ayin" is "`ay-in to-vah" meaning "good eye"; or good will toward others in generosity."[124] Anyone can see and know that doing "mitzvot" or good deeds is the will of God. This is a key component of worshiping the Lord. We do not do good deeds to be saved but rather we do good deeds because we are saved by Yeshua. These are the only good deeds acceptable to God the Father. This is the "good eye" of the Body of Christ.

By faith in God, we know in our hearts that good works in His name are beneficial to us and others in society.

By faith in God, we know in our hearts that good works in His name are beneficial to us and others in society. It does not bring righteousness to us. Yeshua is our righteousness and we see and know to do good works that will glorify the Father in Heaven. Many times good works does involve sharing our wealth and material goods.

The last example of "Ayin" used in a Hebrew word is "`o-lam", which means "eternity; world or everlasting."[125] This word connects to "ha'e-met" which is the world to come in which prophetic truth will prevail.[126] We can laugh at the days to come because we are going into eternity with the Father, Son and Holy Spirit. We are blessed to have the book of Revelation and anyone who reads and believes the prophecies has a good eye ready for the coming of the Messiah, Yeshua the King.

Physical eyes are used to reveal but they rely on the lights reflection. So too, our spiritual eyes rely on the light of Yeshua Messiah to reveal the spiritual realm. We must see into and know by faith in the teachings of Yeshua. He will cloth us in His truth and majesty and we will have eternal joy in the Holy Spirit.

In this proverb, this spiritually rich woman is reflecting the inward God-ordained qualities bestowed upon her. This inwardly adorned female is clothed with strength and dignity. She is clothed in strength because of her active passionate courage. Time and time again, among her husband, children, domestic help, and business associates, her foresight and confidence reveals a woman full of joy and faith. Her peers see a spiritually strong woman.

Strength, used wisely, will overcome potential disasters or impending threatening circumstances.

Strength, used wisely, will overcome potential disasters or impending threatening circumstances. She sees her value and worth are part of her inward clothing. This dignified woman who has struggled to learn God's Torah and apply it to life's situations, inwardly feels the fruition of strength and spiritual laughter. She lives in the palm of God's hand. No matter the situation or emotional response she knows a joy beyond the limits of humanity.

Her inner qualities of strength and dignity reveal a true humility as Yeshua did to his brethren. She is optimistic and confident as she faces life's trials and tribulations. She is firm and consistent in making decisions and deals honorably with all. Her diligence and acknowledgment of God has brought her joy and hope of heart. We read these words in *Ephesians 1:18-19*,

> *"I pray that he will give light to the eyes of your hearts, so that you will understand the hope to which he has called you, what rich glories there are in the inheritance he has promised to his people, and how surpassingly great is his power working in us who trust him."*

Her spirit is alive in the Lord and clothed with godly characteristics. Her confidence and joy is a work of the Holy Spirit and she knows from where her inward power comes. Soon enough, old age will bring its pains and sorrows but her joy will see her through those golden years as she laughs and shouts for joy (*Psalms 126:2a*). She has prepared and her children will continue her legacy of godly nobility. She knows honor will be given to her in future generations as an example to heed and follow. Her exemplary attitude is a testimony to *Philippians 4:13* which says,

"I can do all things through Him who gives me power."

Her children see and have a good reason to honor her *(Exodus 20:12)* because they too can laugh and rejoice in the days to come. No matter the day, whether it is a normal work day or Shabbat and even the appointed Feasts of the Lord, she continues the God ordained journey with her husband and children into the future of aging gracefully. Her beauty may fade and her mind may weaken, but the spirit expresses a heart of delight as she witnesses the spiritual success of her children.

"I will rejoice in Yerushalayim and take joy in my people. The sound of weeping will no longer be heard in it, no longer the sound of crying" (*Isaiah 65:19*).

Every women experiences good times and some not so good. But being clothed with spiritual strength and dignity can help you to see the future and rejoice even in the days to come. This female has prepared as best she can, by God's grace. Strength and dignity comes from an eye of faith and trust in the Lord. It can express itself in a true woman clothed in the love and laughter of God.

The Scriptures teach us to clothe ourselves with the Lord. Physical outward appearances may be enhanced but it is the inward man that needs to be clothed in Yeshua's strength and dignity. The Apostle John saw Yeshua clothed in majesty. We read these words in *Revelation 1:12-15*,

> *"I turned around to see who was speaking to me; and when I had turned, I saw seven gold menorahs; and among the menorahs was someone like a Son of Man, wearing a robe down to his feet and a gold band around his chest. His head and hair were as white as snow-white wool, his eyes like a fiery flame, his feet like burnished brass refined in a furnace, and his voice like the sound of rushing waters."*

We too, by faith and trust in the Lord, adorn ourselves in Him. It is not by our might and strength but by the Spirit of the living God. This proverbial woman has limited her time focusing on herself and has given the Lord His honor and glory. Her character of spirit is reflected into the lives of those around her. Her smile and love of mankind gives her a desire to be joyful in the Lord. Remember these anointed words of the apostle Sha'ul,

> *"Instead, clothe yourselves with the Lord Yeshua the Messiah; and don't waste your time thinking about how to provide for the sinful desires of your old nature." Romans 13:14*

In Him, we can laugh at the enemy and the days to come. Our security rests in Him. Our mouths speak His truth in joy and laughter.

Clothed With Strength

"For you come to meet him with the best blessings, you place a crown of fine gold on his head. He asks you for life; you give it to him, years and years forever and ever." (Psalms 21:4(3)-5(4))

Let Us Reason Together

Describe the last difficult situation when you needed to use wisdom. What was the end result?

What steps do you need to take to obtain more wisdom?

Is your outside or inside appearance more important? (Before you respond, think carefully!)

How would your spouse respond to that question about you?

What are your spiritual strengths? Describe what it means to be spiritually wrapped in strength and dignity.

As each day approaches, can you see without worry?

What questions, thoughts, or feelings do you have after reading chapter sixteen?

NOTES

NOTES

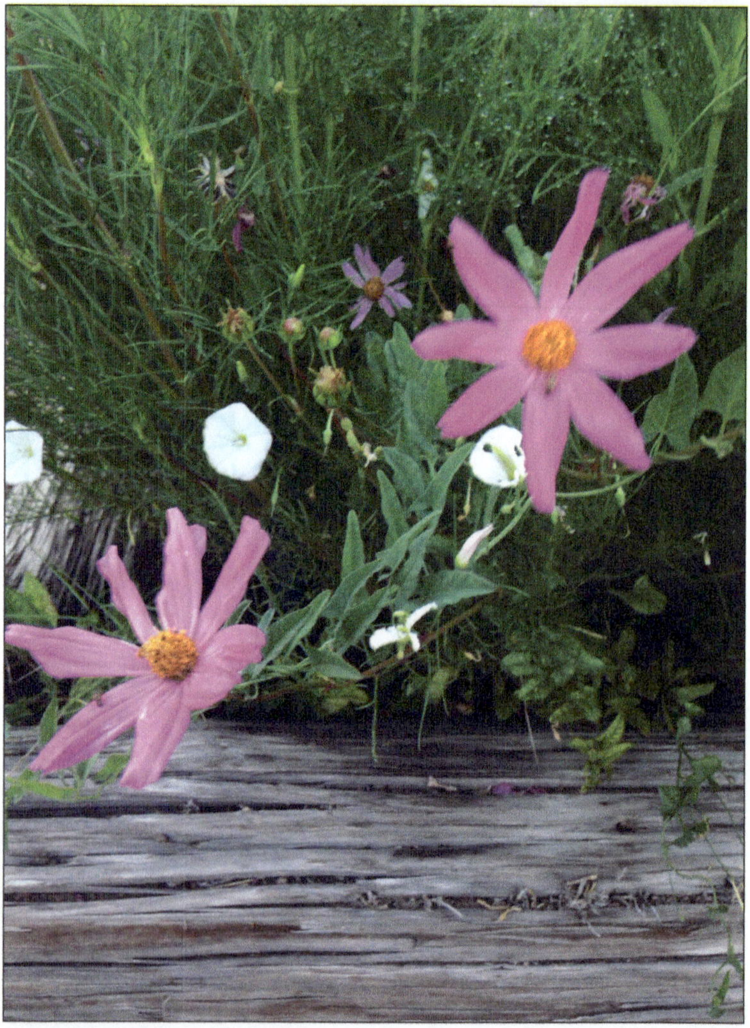

Chapter 17

WHEN SHE OPENS

"When she opens her mouth, she speaks wisely; on her tongue is loving instruction." (Proverbs 31:26)

"The seventeenth letter of the Hebrew alphabet is called "Pey" (pronounced "pay").[127] It has the sound of "p" as in "pain."[128] Its pictographic form represents a "mouth"[129] The symbolic meanings are "to speak, or open"[130], "work or speech."[131] The mouth was primarily created to communicate to God.[132] Words can work to encourage or destroy a person's spirit. Much can be conveyed with this letter "Pey" in conceptual spiritual realities. To know the Lord is to use the right words at the proper time in all circumstances. This can only be achieved with a heartfelt intense study and hearing of God's Word. His love and truth will give one the anointed words to speak.

A Hebrew word using the letter "Pey" is called "pu-rim" which is a national day in Israel called "Purim". It is celebrated in Jewish communities worldwide. It commemorates the salvation of the Jews from Haman the Agagi who wanted to murder all the Jewish people in the known world.[133] This story is found in the book of ***Esther***. A beautiful Jewish girl speaking the anointed intercessory words of salvation to the king, as she wisely works to save her people from annihilation. She is given control of the future by the king due to her respectful and heartfelt speech. Esther used wisdom for "such a time as this" (***Esther 4:14***).

Another Hebrew word, endearing to my heart, using "Pey" is "pe-sach". This translates to Pesach; Passover.[134] The most famous and celebrated Feast of the Lord commemorates the salvation of Israel as she is delivered, by the hand of God, from Egyptian slavery. Eventually the Feast is discovered to be a foreshadow of Yeshua's death as the Passover Lamb. God spoke His salvation to mankind by sacrificing His only begotten Son who worked to willingly give us His life as a bloody, acceptable to God, sacrificial death.

Lastly, "pil-pul" which means; debate regarding legal matters on religious questions[135] requires wise words spoken in order to achieve Godly rulings. The religious leaders of Israel constantly spoke the Torah and debated the interpretations until acceptable oral traditions were agreed upon for the most part.

In this proverb, we discover a female who has a way with kind spoken words of wisdom. Everything that is spoken from her mouth proves she has a heart of wisdom and passionate love of trying to resolve the situation or discussion. To speak with wisdom while giving loving instruction is a true gift of the Lord. To speak wisely means a woman has contemplated first, in her spirit, the Torah. Her righteous loving mind processes the spiritual realities and then she gives voice in sounds that echo concepts of God's truth and will. When she begins to speak, those around her listen intently for the voice of God.

Loving speech can build a home's spiritual environment to the glory of God or work negatively to tear a family apart.

A person can speak thoughtful words of wisdom or rash pragmatic words of destruction. Loving speech can build a home's spiritual environment to the glory of God or work negatively to tear a family apart. It is imperative to have an attitude of praying to the Lord for wisdom when using the mouth to speak. Think and judge your words before using them rashly.

God's spoken Word guides the footsteps of a noble woman as she uses His Word to guide her husband and children. Her social skills will eventually bring her the honor and respect above all women. *"Your words are a doorway that lets in light, giving understanding to the thoughtless. My mouth is wide open, as I pant with longing for your mitzvot."* (***Psalms 119:130-131***).

In my experiences of life, I have had the blessed opportunity to hear wise women speak to me whether lovingly or with aggressive impassioned rebuke. A godly wise proverbial woman knows that wise words and loving instruction have a parameter of kind gentleness to righteous "loving" anger. A virtuous woman, prior to speaking, has asked God to "hand select" approved words of wisdom that can be effective at the right moment in the right frame of spirit and mind.

> *"Set a guard, Adonai, over my mouth; keep watch at the door of my lips" (Psalms 141:3).*

This particular proverb gives testimony to her speech. It is wise and points to an end result of defined instruction with the expectation of respected results. As she opens her mouth to speak, there is kindness and empathy whether speaking directly to a person or about them to others. Boldness, love and faith in Yeshua should be incorporated into spoken words. She is working to build the community and the nation of Israel.

The tongue is the main organ of speech and the tongue should be speaking "a law of kindness".[136] Words work to create blessing or cursings upon ourselves or those around us. As people listen to our speech it reveals our character whether righteous or questionable. We cannot tame our tongues. But I know who can tame the tongue with His Spirit. Ask the Lord for this blessing. A Christ-like atmosphere will develop by godly speech.

> *"By the word of Adonai the heavens were made, and their whole host by a breath from his mouth" (Psalms 33:6).*

Speaking God's truth will make you a respected peer to younger generations. A noble wife is a spokeswoman of the Lord. Her speech is clean and sanctified as she skillfully transfers her spiritual voice to the physical world of language. She is the opposite of a spiritually distant and empty heart. We read this truth in *Isaiah 29:13a*,

"Then Adonai said: Because these people approach me with empty words, and the honor they bestow on me is mere lip-service; while in fact they have distanced their hearts from me..."

Good words benefit and are helpful to the family and the community. Family members want to be loved with kind and wise words that have been crafted from the Torah. Reading and speaking the Word of God will develop the skills necessary to speak loving instruction. Your primary communication should be to your Savior but, you are to speak His words of loving instruction to those He has in your care.

> *"Let no harmful language come from your mouth, only good words that are helpful in meeting the need, words that will benefit those who hear them"* (*Ephesians 4:29*).

Slander and obscene talk destroy those around you, as well as your reputation. We have all abused our blessings of speech but today is a new day to repent and turn to God for the proper use of our tongues.

As she opens her mouth to speak, a dignified wife is going to express a mastery of Psalms, Proverbs, and Ecclesiastes. Divine words to summon her listeners for a full righteous and religious discourse.[137] She will speak good practical common sense instruction that is reliable and loving.[138] Insight into the holiness of God will be experienced by her and the listeners (***Proverbs 2:1-5***).

Loving instruction is a great blessing. Females have a special gift of love as they speak words of wisdom and knowledge of Yeshua Messiah. Building reliable relationships requires loving wise instruction and encouragement. Fervent passion and kinship can be revealed in thought, speech, and deed. King David, prior to his crowning, spoke with elegance and respect to God's anointed out-going King Shaul. He found favor with the son of the king, Y'honatan. David's wise words caught the attention of those who heard him speak. By the time David had finished speaking to Sha'ul, Y'honatan found himself inwardly drawn by David's character, so that Y'honatan loved him as he did himself" (***1 Samuel 18:1***).

Of course as readers of the Scriptures know, Yeshua Messiah is the perfect representation of the letter "Pey". Throughout the Gospels we discover He spoke only what His Father told Him to speak. The Holy Spirit directed His every thought, word and deed. Every letter spoken from His mouth generated perfect wisdom and righteous instruction. Anyone who truly had a heart to repent received His perfect love and attention. His words spoke life from the dead and healed thousands with various physical infirmities. His spoken words gained the attention of multiple thousands upon thousands. Everyone came to hear Him and only Him. His salvific words caught thousands of lost souls and harvested those dead in their sins.

Everyone needs godly instruction that is wise and loving. Ultimately an honorable wife uses speech that is controlled by God's love and is good-hearted. A true spontaneous act that can one day be used to catch a soul for Yeshua Messiah. With her verbal love she truly is a watchman of the Lord.

> *"the twenty-four elders fall down before the One sitting on the throne, who lives forever and ever, and worship him. They throw their crowns in front of the throne." (Revelation 4:10)*

Let Us Reason Together

What is your typical response when you are under pressure or in the fire?

How often do you check your own vocabulary?

Are you speaking words of love, compassion and thoughtful correction or are you speaking frustration?

What can you do before you verbally explode and leave a negative image?

When you hear someone speaking calmly in a difficult situation how do you view that person?

What questions, thoughts, or feelings do you have after reading chapter seventeen?

NOTES

NOTES

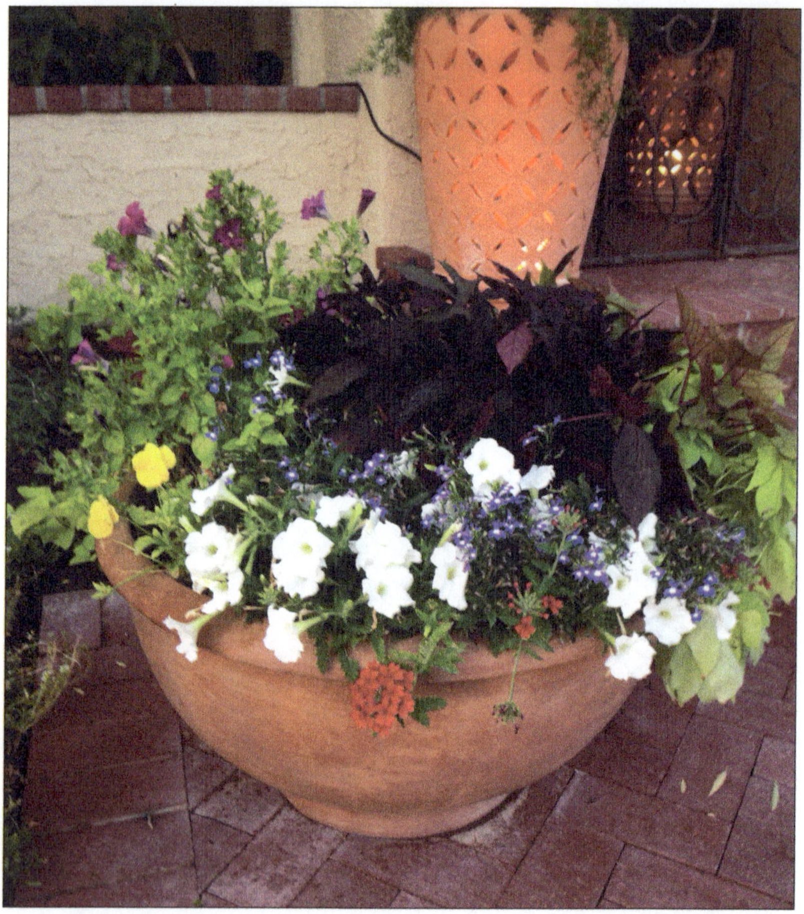

Chapter 18

SHE WATCHES

"She watches how things go in her house, not eating the bread of idleness." (Proverbs 31:27)

"The eighteenth letter of the Hebrew alphabet is called "Tsade" (pronounced "tsah-dee").[139] It has the sound of "ts" as in "bolts".[140] The pictorial representation is a 'fish-hook"[141] or "a two handed sickle."[142] The symbolic meaning is "need or harvest."[143] Other related representations are to catch, take captive or harvesting the righteous. As the Holy Spirit captivates our hearts and begins to speak to us, we must catch the moment with our reverent hearts for salvation and harvest the lost for Yeshua Messiah.

A Hebrew word using the letter "Tsade" is "tsad-diq" which means a pious, just and righteous man.[144] Show me such a one, and I will show you a willing student ready to be taken captive by their Lord and Savior Yeshua Messiah. Another Hebrew word is "tsur yisra'el" means "Rock of Israel."[145] It is a name of God. Yeshua Messiah is the Rock of Israel and is the ultimate Fisher of men, ready to harvest the spirits of men into a new life with the Holy Spirit. Open your heart to Yeshua and let Him captivate your heart and fulfill every need in your life.

> *"Yeshua said to them, '"Come after me, and I will make you fishers for men!' "At once they left their nets and went with him"* (*Matthew 4:19-20*).

The Hebrew word "tsi-yon" means "Zion."[146] It is the city of David which refers to the Temple Mount and Jerusalem. This city was not built by idle Jews, but with their reverent faith in Adonai and their blood, sweat and tears. It is a city full of pious servants of God with spiritual needs. Today thousands upon thousands come to Jerusalem humbly seeking Yeshua and petitioning Him for themselves and loved ones. The Lord does not sit idly by watching His beloved. He is ever making intercession for the saints.

The home is the frontline of spiritual harvesting and she is not going to allow an indolent lifestyle to develop in her home.

This proverb is a great testimony of a noble wife exercising strength over her household. The home is the frontline of spiritual harvesting and she is not going to allow an indolent lifestyle to develop in her home. Her watchful eye catches the members of the household. A wise female watches and she knows the difference between rest and idleness. She has a strong sense of perception and discernment and at any given moment the temptation of idleness will cause her to establish a decisive decision at the proper time and place.

Life is a constant act of worship to God, even on Shabbat the day to rest. A home is a dwelling for a family but it is also a place to take captive for the glory of God. Therefore, before she reacts to any situation in the home, she will study the moment and guide herself and those who occupy the house. Her first spiritual harvest is going to be her children. Her spiritual nurture will be the fishhook to catch the hearts of the children and teach them reverence and hard work for the Lord.

The wife is keeping covenant with God and she knows idleness can lead to discontent and self-pity.

"She watches," means "alertness as a watchman"[147] and this is a process that is followed day in and day out as the affairs of the family are played out. The wife is keeping covenant with God and she knows idleness can lead to discontent and self-pity. Therefore, observation over the home and necessary ruler-ship protects the spiritual, intellectual and emotional condition of her family from digression. She is always in a guarded condition just as God guarded His own. Her prostrate spirit is always in prayer for her family. She is not going to allow slothfulness to catch and captivate her family. She knows an idle mind is open to evil lazy activity that tries to arouse her children. But this spiritual giant knows the enemy must be dealt with immediately.

> *"But the Lord is worthy of trust; he will make you firm and guard you from the Evil One" (2 Thessalonians 3:3).*

The household needs a worshipful female to shepherd the children and domestic servants. Domestic affairs such as feeding the family, clothing their bodies, seeking medical treatments or teaching the young responsibilities will prove fruitful to the grateful husband. He knows an effective functioning home is the result of a strong motivated wife.

The noble wife is not going to allow herself or those under her authority to eat or partake spiritually, intellectually or physically the fruit of idleness or latent activity. Not even Shabbat will be used for idleness and irresponsibility. It will be a day to rest but also a day to honor the Lord. No member of the home is going to be unserviceable or worthless. She along with all members of the home are not going to nullify active responsibility.

> *"About an hour before sundown, he went out, found still others standing around, and asked them, 'Why have you been standing here all day, doing nothing?" They said to him, 'Because no one hired*

us.' 'You too,' He told them, 'go to the vineyard.'
Matthew 20:6-7

The day was almost ending and the owner of the vineyard used workers to the best advantage for his harvest, and the workers themselves. So too, a watchful wife and mother knows the task at hand and will displace idleness and laziness by delegating duties to the household. Preplanning is the key to harvesting a full day of successful education, work and business. The alert wife's home does not entertain poor leadership and idleness.

All children, for the most part, and the hired help can at times be inclined not to do work. But not under a noble woman's watchful eye. She will voice a proverb and teach her listeners a lesson. Idle children are but a symptom of a neglectful mother. There are times of recreation but it needs to be limited. Mankind was not created to play all day. Productive employment and a hard work ethic is the will of God.

"Go to the ant you lazybones! Consider its ways, and be wise" (Proverbs 6:6).

A slothful wife hesitates and is negligent in chores such as Torah study, education and Gospel outreach. The home is a place to live, study, learn and worship God together. It is a busy place and at proper moments it is a place to rest and relax. But sluggards lose understanding of spiritual truths due to idleness in Scripture studies. The righteous woman is not going to have any sluggard or idle mind living under the same roof with her and her husband. A lazy life can be a reflection of a lazy spirit. These words we read in *1 Corinthians 3:13*,

"But each one's work will be shown for what it is; the Day will disclose it, because it will be revealed by fire-the fire will test the quality of each one's work."

We are to be useful and productive and a noble wife will ensure her family partakes of the pleasure in duty and the blessing of having a home and community to live in. Her children have a good leader to follow as a great example of a pious saint.

"Grandchildren are the crown of the aged, while the glory of children is their ancestors." (Proverbs 17:6)

Let Us Reason Together

How would your spouse describe your work habits?

Take a few moments and describe yourself. Are you a slave driver, an ethical worker, a work-aholic, lazy, persistent etc?

How can you bring balance into your life? Into your spouse's life?

With what kind of protection do you cover your family? Is this protection obvious to others?

What steps do you need to take to improve your concept of a balanced life?

Is idleness an issue in your home? Are your children being productive in household duties?

What questions, thoughts or feelings do you have after reading chapter eighteen?

NOTES

NOTES

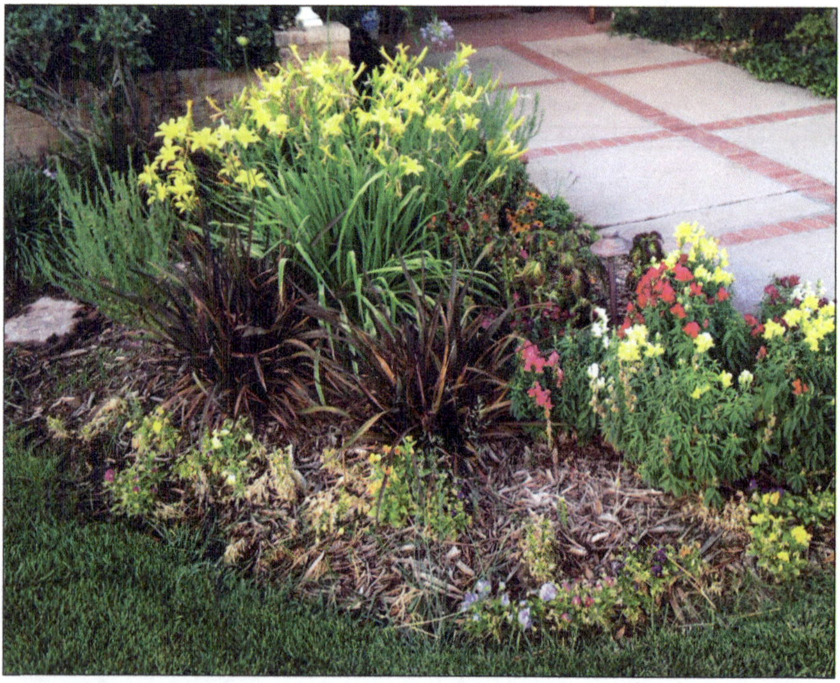

Chapter 19

HER CHILDREN ARISE

"Her children arise; they make her happy; her husband too, as he praises her." (Proverbs 31:28)

"The nineteenth letter of the Hebrew alphabet is called "Qof" (pronounced "kof") and has the sound of "q" as in "queen".[148] Its pictographic Hebrew shape represents the "back of the head,"[149] or "sun on the horizon."[150] Its symbolic meaning is "behind, the last."[151] This proverbial midrash will focus on the symbolic representation of the importance of knowing the back of someone's head.

A Hebrew word using the letter "Kof" is "qo-desh haq-qo da-shim" which translates to "The Holy of Holies."[152] This was where the Ark of the Covenant was placed. The back of the head was the last thing the Israelites saw in the great leadership the High Priest, as he entered the Holy Place prior to entering the Holy of Holies. He was leading Israel in the ultimate act of worship on the High and Holy Day that occurred once a year.

Another Hebrew word is "qo-he-let" which is the book of *Ecclesiastes*.[153] As King Solomon saw the sun on the horizon day after day he came to some anointed conclusions about man's life on this earth. Futility and meaninglessness pervade the mind and life's existence if a person does not follow and worship the Lord Almighty. The rich and poor end up in the same place if they do not acknowledge God. Life is meaningless and without God to follow and learn from, there is no point to go on living. Mankind will arise each day to only see another day of watching the sun go down on the horizon without God. But, hope and belief in the Lord Yeshua will make each day worth getting up for, to His glory and honor.

Because children are confident that their mother is directing their path to success, it will give them confidence in her leadership.

In this proverb, we see evidence of what follows as a result of following. Children will always follow someone or something and if they are not as familiar with the back of the mothers head as well the front of her head, there can be a setup for failure. Because children are confident that their mother is directing their path to success, it will give them confidence in her leadership. Follow me, as I follow Yeshua Messiah should be a mothers belief as a great role model for her husband and children. We read these words of confidence in leadership in *1 Corinthians 10:31-11:1*

"Well, whatever you do, whether it's eating or drinking or anything else, do it all so as to bring glory to God. Do not be an obstacle to anyone-not to Jews, not to Gentiles, and not to God's Messianic Community. Just as I try to please everyone in everything I do, not looking out for my own interests but for those of the many, so that they may be saved; try to imitate me, even as I myself try to imitate the Messiah."

Her example of knowing the Torah and living in a relationship to the Lord, is an example that leads the children as they follow her and see the back of a great spiritual leader's head. This in turn will teach them to honor their mother. Her happiness will be achieved as she watches them follow her with respect and love.

It is okay to be following a great leader and great leaders are great followers. A righteous wife is an important spiritual leader in the home. It is imperative the wife and mother should be aware she is being followed, and therefore ensures the back of her head is a visual sign to the children that she expects to be followed by them as she follows the Lord.

Another thing we began to see in this proverb is that the fruit of righteousness begins to appear in a noble female as the end of **Proverbs 31** comes to a close. The last proverbs in this proverbial prophecy, speak her praise starting with this letter "Kof". This is a result of her faithfulness to God which in turn is manifested in faithfulness to her husband and children. She is praised because she is also a follower. Her leader is the Lord Almighty.

Wisdom and nobleness of character "inspire praises from the family".[154] Those who know her best arise and make her happy. Starting with the children, they work through effort to bring her honor and happiness due to her wonderful love and care of them. The children are well aware they are loved unconditionally and their hearts have nothing but love and a desire to please their mother.

All through life the child has looked into this mother's eyes and were recipients of her wisdom, love, protection and nourishment. She represents, in living flesh, the love of God. Their eyes and bodies have followed her their whole lives. They could recognize her from the back of her head. As the children grow, they too will become that spiritual leader who teaches their own children what the back of their head looks like each day as the sun rises and sets. In **Psalms 127:3-5** we find these words,

> *Children too are a gift from Adonai; the fruit of the womb is a reward. The children born when one is young, are like arrows in the hand of a warrior. How blessed is the man who has filled his quiver with them; he will not have to be embarrassed when contending with foes at the city gate."*

A blessed child is blessed to have a righteous mother who is noble in the Word of God. They follow her and in turn are a blessing to their father at the city gates. The sun will set on the horizon and it will be another day of infamy as her children declare her praises to her and their peers. Even the husband will sing her praise at the city gates and among the elders. Inclusive to honoring the mother with praise so too the husband gives joy of heart, a voice of praise for his beloved wife. He speaks well of her because he is fortunate and envied by his peers for having such a woman as a wife. True thanksgiving for a wonderful wife and mother will be verbal public recognition with the utmost love.

"As for husbands, love your wives, just as the Messiah loved the Messianic Community, indeed, gave himself up on its behalf" (Ephesians 5:25).

The disciples of Yeshua are to follow Him and learn the back of His head. In Hebrew the word "talmidim" means disciples. The twelve followed Him all over Israel. When He moved as the pillar of fire moved in the wilderness so too the disciples moved. When He stopped they stopped. A Rabbi has students following them. They do not step in front of their teacher but respectfully follow their beloved leader. They know the back of their Rabbi's head. Due to Yeshua's love and salvation the worship and praises of Him by His disciples make Him happy.

> *"You, my sheep, the sheep in my pasture, are human beings; and I am your God,' says Adonai Elohim"* (*Ezekiel 34:31*).

As we spiritually fellowship and follow the Shepherd, we will begin to know Him more intimately through our faith in Him. This in turn will cause us to arise each day and give thanks and praise for His eternal love and salvation at the city gates.

> *"Always give thanks for everything to God the Father in the name of our Lord Yeshua the Messiah"* (*Ephesians 5:20*).

In this proverb, the family is able to sing her praises and in doing so, it gives her a place of highest of honor in the hearts of the husband and children. A mother who is faithful is worthy of the highest of honor we can give under God's authority. She is a person of highest honor among the women in the community.

> *"On that day, Adonai-Tzva'ot will be a glorious crown, a brilliant diadem for the remnant of his people."* (*Isaiah 28:5*)

Let Us Reason Together

When was the last time you showed leadership in your home? In the community? Describe the situations.

What strengths do you possess as a leader? What strengths does your spouse possess?

How can your strengths and weaknesses compliment your spouse's?

Who follows your lead?

What can you do to improve your weakest areas?

What questions, thoughts, or feelings do you have after reading chapter nineteen?

NOTES

NOTES

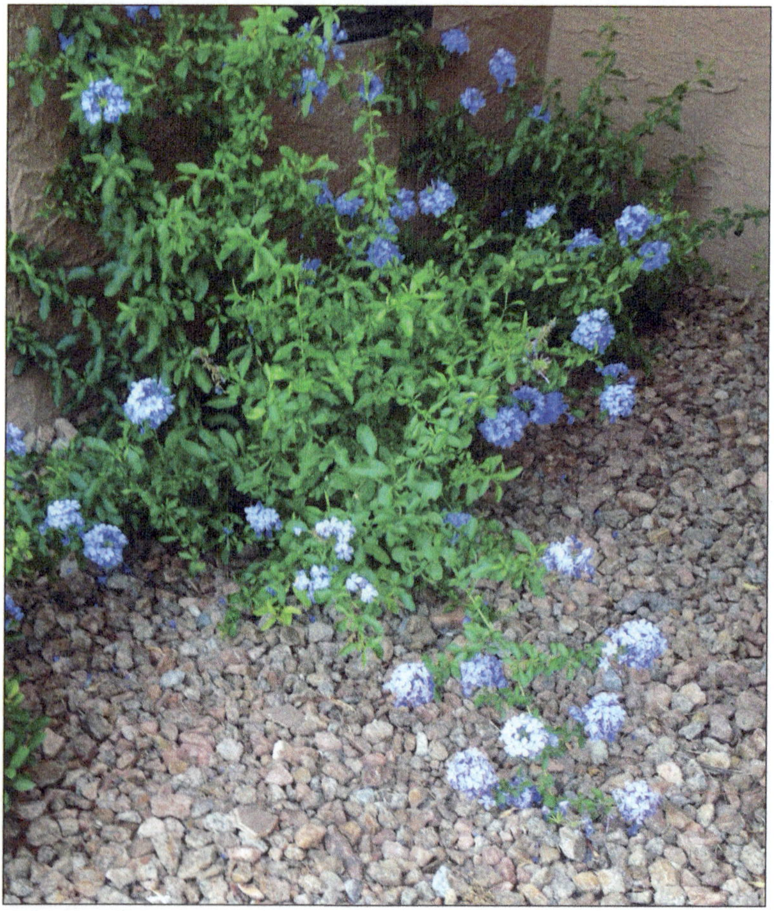

Chapter 20

MANY WOMEN

"Many women have done wonderful things, but you surpass them all!" (Proverbs 31:29)

"The twentieth letter of the Hebrew alphabet is called "Resh" (pronounced "raysh") and has the sound of "r" as in "relationship."[155] As you pronounce the "r" it is done by rolling the tongue just as you would do it with words in Spanish. The pictorial shape represents a human "head."[156] The symbolic meaning is a "person or highest."[157]

In this blessed proverb, the focus is on a particular person of highest interest as we approach the closing of this brilliant and anointed prophecy by a mother (***Proverbs 31:1***). God wants his highest and best for such a faithful women due to her godliness and faithfulness to Yehovah and in turn her husband and children.

A beautiful Hebrew word using the letter "Resh" is "ru-ach" which means "wind, breathe or air."[158] More importantly this word is connected to the Spirit of the living God; namely God the Holy Spirit is the reference here. The Father wants all mankind to be touched and filled by His Spirit to achieve His highest and best will for their lives. If an individual treats the Holy Spirit on the highest level of their faith they can be filled supernaturally with the characteristics of the Spirit of God. The Holy Spirit came on the Feast of Weeks (Shavu'ot) as promised by our Savior Yeshua Messiah when He said He would send the Comforter to all the believers in Him. *Acts 2:1-4* shares these words,

> *"The festival of Shavu`ot arrived, and the believers all gathered together in one place. Suddenly there came a sound from the sky like the roar of a violent wind, and it filled the whole house where they were sitting. Then they saw what looked like tongues of fire, which separated and came to rest on each one of them. They were all filled with the Ruach Ha`kodesh and began to talk in different languages, as the Spirit enabled them to speak."*

Another Hebrew word is "Rut."[159] Her name means "close friend or mate."[160] This is the most romantic love story between and man and a woman that one can find in the whole of Scriptures. It is a foreshadow of the greater Lover who would save Israel and the whole world from the results of sin by redemption. He, Yeshua, would become a believers Kinsman Redeemer. Ruth, the Moabite widow, came to faith in the God of Israel through the Jewish people. She achieved the highest will of God by becoming His child, through obeying and listening to the Jewish people share their faith and trust in the Torah. She became a person of highest honor among the Jewish people. The royal bloodline of Israel would be her prodigy. Here are her words as she rebukes her mother-in-law who's trying to tell her to go back to her pagan people,

> *"But Rut said",'Don't press me to leave you and stop following you; for wherever you go, I will go; and wherever you stay, I will stay. Your people will be my people and your God will be my God. Where you die, I will die; and there I will be buried. May Adonai bring terrible curses on me, and worse ones as well, if anything but death separates you and me'"* (*Ruth 1:16-17*)

The last example of using the letter "Resh" in a Hebrew word is "ro-`eh" which means "Shepherd; leader."[161] **Psalm 23** is the infamous biblical psalm for all the saints of God concerning their highest leader. One day we will see our Shepherd perfectly face to face. But now we are seeing Him letter by letter. If we obey and follow the highest person, Yeshua, we are true Hebrew sons and daughters because we crossed over to a new life in Him.

In this proverb, the husband recognizes many women who have done great things but he praises her above them all.

In this proverb, the husband recognizes many women who have done great things but he praises her above them all. She is a true a Hebrew and Israelite of the highest sort. Not to discount biblical women of faith in God or even her contemporaries, this husband believes his wife has surpassed them all as he praises her in the ultimate highest honor. He is shouting to the world in the city of Zion that his wife is the highest wife a man could ever be married to. So on behalf of God, himself, and the children he gives a poetic voice of praise to her. You are the best. You are the finest. You're the highest in my heart and home. He was not idolizing her but simply giving voice through joy in his heart for her. **Romans 13:7b** tells us,

> *"If you owe someone respect, pay him respect; if you owe someone honor, pay him honor."*

Among the Israelite community of women, the husband ensures his faithful and deeply devout wife is placed among the honorable women of society. Her efforts will ensure the name of her husband's honor will be continuous into future generations (**Numbers 27:1-11**). The wonderful things such as raising godly children and developing a business to supplement the finances of the home are worthy of honor. But it is her devotion to God and living in His righteousness that has caused her husband to bless her in his highest efforts.

Again, the things she has done are not inclusive to only the confines of the home but in the business community affairs. Her godly skills and faithfulness to God have given God the opportunity to do marvelous things in and through her. This in turn causes those to praise Adonai and honor her accordingly.

An element of "wonderful things" is the ability of a woman to lead people to the true and living Savior. A righteous, excellent and loyal wife will be a high spiritual leader among women. She is endowed with spiritual gifts that transcend human possibilities. Her trust in God's salvation is shared to those who listen to her wisdom. She experiences from God, *Isaiah 43:4*, and this makes her a woman of high regard to look upon.

> *"Because I regard you as valued and honored, and because I love you. For you I will give people, nations in exchange for your life"* (*Isaiah 43:4*).

The family has experienced a love from their wife and mother that surpasses human comprehension. In turn, she is recognized at the highest of respect and adoration possible by her husband. In *Ephesians 3:17b-19* we read these sacred words that a righteous woman has prayed over her family,

> *"Also I pray that you will be rooted and founded in love, so that you, with all God's people, will be given strength to grasp the breadth, length, height and*

> ***depth of the Messiah's love, yes, to know it, even though it's beyond all knowing, so that you will be filled with all the fullness of God."***

Yeshua is the perfect representation of the letter "Resh". He is the highest person who has done the most wonderful thing humanity could ever or will ever attempt to achieve. He has surpassed every human being that was created. No one will ever surpass our Savior in knowledge, power, and position. Ever. Scriptures testify of Him in the Law, Prophets, and Writings. The New Covenant reveals Yeshua as Savior and the way to eternal life. All of our praises and glorious worship are directed toward Him as we eternally thank Him for so rich a salvation.

Truthfully, a woman of excellent character who has dedicated her whole life to the glory of Yeshua is but a woman whom God has poured His supernatural grace upon. She stands, in the hearts of her husband and children, as the highest of women. Her resolve to be a success in the home and in society has brought honor to whom honor is due. This proverb depicts the strongest of emotions to express the highest praise a man can give to a noble wife. This will destroy the temptation to honor outward beauty over inward godly goodness.

> ***"Surrounding the throne were twenty-four other thrones, and on the thrones sat twenty-four elders***

dressed in white clothing and wearing gold crowns on their heads." (Revelation 4:4)

Let Us Reason Together

How much trust, honor and praise do you offer to your spouse?

What does God's supernatural grace look like in your life today?

Encouragement is contagious! What steps must you take to become this *Proverbs 31* woman?

What marvelous things is God working in and through you?

What questions, thoughts, or feelings do you have after reading chapter twenty?

NOTES

NOTES

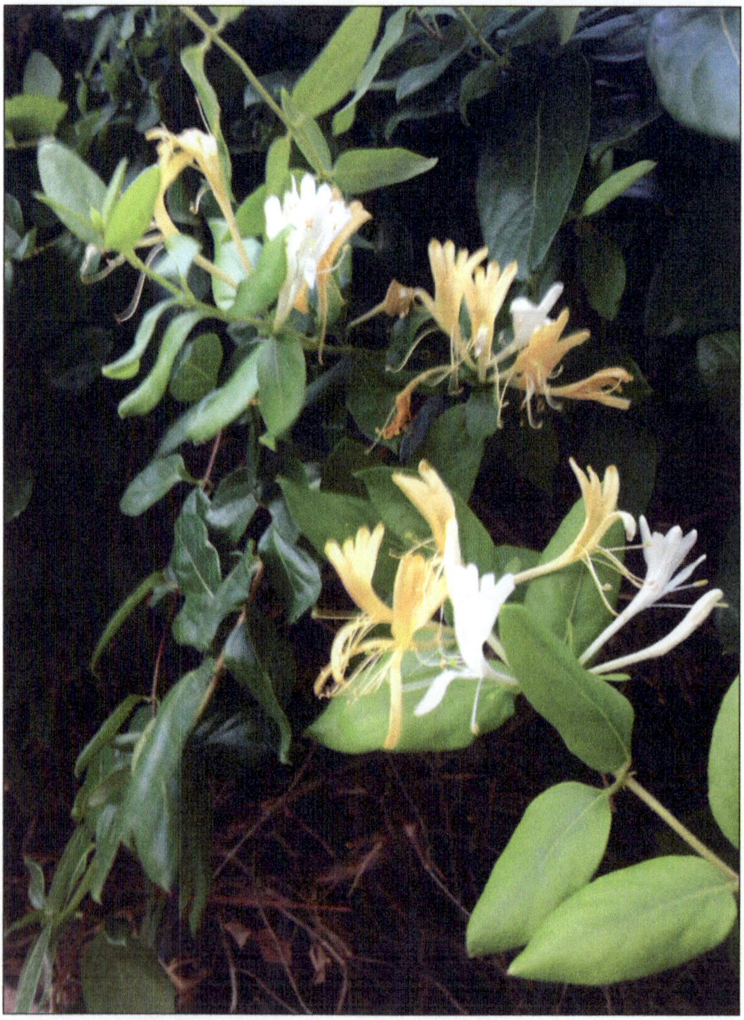

Chapter 21

CHARM CAN LIE

"Charm can lie, beauty can vanish, but a woman who fears Adonai should be praised." (Proverbs 31:30).

"The twenty-first letter of the Hebrew alphabet is called "Shin" (pronounced "sheen") and has the sound of "sh" as in "sheep."[162] It also carries the "s" sound as in "stop." The pictorial shape represents "teeth"[163] or "mouth"[164] and the symbolic meaning is "consume, or destroy."[165] The absence of shalom (peace) is chaos and we need revelation of God's Word in order to destroy chaos and its cause. Another possible symbolic meaning is the manifestation of God to destroy chaos.[166]

Anything that endeavors to rise above the Lord Almighty, whether in life or in the spiritual realm, is to be destroyed. The ability of the flesh and mind can convince an individual of its exaggerated value and strength. Our minds and flesh are limited in ability because they eventually are corrupted by humanism, time, age or disease. People can use charm or looks to achieve aspects of selfishness and greed but the reverence for God can destroy this deception.

There are numerous words in Hebrew that use the letter "Shin." One is "sha-vu-`ot" which is the feast of the Lord translated as Feast of Weeks.[167] This feast, in the April and May timeframe, honors God by offering Him the first fruits of harvest and trusting Him for a bountiful year of produce. His approved blessing will consume and destroy poverty and hunger that could result from a famine or plague in the land of Israel. Due to Israel obeying the Lord, the blessings of rain at the proper times would bring prosperity to the nation.

Another well-known Hebrew word is "shab-bat."[168] Shabbat is the seventh day of the week in which all saints are to rest, worship, observe and meditate upon Lord. This day will destroy exhaustion of spirit, mind and body. This is one of the Ten Words of the Lord. We read these words in **Exodus 20:8**,

"Remember the day, Shabbat, to set it apart for God."

One sad word using "Shin" in Hebrew is "sho-'ah" which means destruction or catastrophe like the Nazi Holocaust during world WWII.[169] The horrific destruction and catastrophe of millions of Jewish people all over Europe was indeed a dark time in history. May the Lord protect Israel by His "she-khi-nah", which means glorious divine presence,[170] from all her enemies.

In this proverb, the holy fear of God, which is faith in Yeshua, and godly character are a women's true strength.[171] Fear of God is the beginning of wisdom and "the ultimate glory of a human being is to stand perpetually in His presence."[172] Her holy fear of God will help establish the spiritual attitudes and foundation of the home. Physical beauty and charm are not the foundational strengths of the home. These attitudes need to be destroyed so inward character is developed righteously.

Young men look predominately to outward beauty and they lose themselves in a clouded confusing world of lust and fascination with female flesh.

Charm and physical beauty can bring chaos and deception. Young men look predominately to outward beauty and they lose themselves in a clouded confusing world of lust and fascination with female flesh. A woman who uses her charm or her beauty as a means to an end, can easily deceive and captivate a future husband without revealing her inward spiritual status or condition.

> *"Pointless! Pointless!–Says Kohelet- Utterly meaningless! Nothing matters" (Ecclesiastes 1:2)*!

But in the end there is hope. We read the ending of ***Ecclesiastes 12:13***,

> *"Here is the final conclusion, now that you have heard everything: fear God, and keep His mitzvot; this is what being human is all about."*

The ability of a female to arouse a man can be deceptive if used to gain favor. Charm is fascinating nothingness for it will dazzle and it is crafty conduct unworthy to God. The Scriptures speak against its use in gaining relationships.

> *"Mouth grandiosities of nothingness, they play on the desires of the old nature, in order to seduce with debaucheries people who have just begun to escape from those whose way of life is wrong"* (2 Peter 2:18).

This passage is one of numerous that depicts the use of charm among unsuspecting or undiscerning individuals. Charm is a way to achieve self-desires by seduction in words and deeds. It can be used as a lie in courting and marriage. The reason it can be a way of lying is because a female can prevaricate when it comes to revealing her spiritual condition. But a noble wife is a women who did not charm and lie herself into a man's heart. This quality will destroy chaos later on in the marriage. Charm and lying are means to seduce and entangle the unsuspecting into spiritual and emotional chaos. They delude people's minds and it becomes a worthless act that will haunt a marital relationship for years to come.

Having womanly beauty is liberating and it can be used to achieve wealth and prestige. Beautiful women are treated and respected more favorably in society. They are pleasant to look at and the unsuspecting do not realize beauty can be a charm that will vanish. But the godly husband knows and see's the inward beauty of fearing Adonai is worthy above the flesh. Being a woman of grace and walking in His purity is true beauty in His essence.

<u>A wise husband reminds his wife it is not charm and beauty that cause him and the children to sing praises to her. Rather, it is the wife who fears the Lord that should be praised.</u>

In Micah 6:8, we read, "Human being, you have already been told what is good, what Adonai demands *of you- no more than to act justly, love grace and walk in purity with your God."*

To a female beauty is important. She wants to look and feel her very best. Wives loved to be called beautiful by their husbands and beauty is appealing in the business world. A wise husband reminds his wife it is not charm and beauty that cause him and the children to sing praises to her. Rather, it is the wife who fears the Lord that should be praised.

Fear of God is an active part of worship to Him. She consistently and prudently guards her life in order to be cautious in outside relationships. She is a reverent and worshipful saint who adores Yeshua.

She respects the rulers and prophets of the land of Israel. This is true fearful worship in The Spirit.

> *"But the time is coming- indeed, it's here now- when the true worshippers will worship the Father spiritually and truly, for these are the kind of people the Father wants worshipping Him" (John 4:23).*

Any wife who conscientiously is devout to the Lord and venerates His beloved Son, Yeshua, is worthy of respect and praise from her husband and children. She does not primarily seek praise of men but rather she seeks the heartbeat of God's kingdom. Her life ultimately is in service to God as we find in **Hebrews 12:28-29**,

> *"Therefore, since we have received an unshakable Kingdom, let us have grace, through which we may offer service that will please God, with reverence and fear. For indeed, "Our God is a consuming fire!"*

This woman who trusts in God rather than charm or beauty is worthy of praise and she is one who will hear one day at the judgment seat of Christ, ***"'Excellent! You are a good and trustworthy servant"*** (***Matthew 25:21***).

My example of choosing a woman, whom I believe to be a great role model to the letter "Shin" in this proverb is a woman in the Bible who struggled with inward chaos and had to find a way to destroy it. This true life narrative is found in the book of *Genesis chapters 27-30*.

Ya'akov (Jacob) was stealthily sent to his mother's family because his brother Esau hated him and wanted to kill him (*Genesis 27*). When Ya'akov arrived in Haran he found Lavan's daughter, Rachel. She was good looking and had beautiful features. Ya'akov fell in love with her. But Rachel had an older sister whose name was Le'ah. Le'ah was not beautiful but through a deceiving act Lavan had Ya'akov marry Le'ah first and then eventually he got married to his true love Rachel.

Le'ah was a secondary unloved wife. She had no beauty to combat Rachel's good looks. Her husband Ya'akov never wanted to marry her but through family cultural honor, he had to in order to marry Rachel. Charm and beauty was no avail to Le'ah and her only hope was God's favor. Eventually Le'ah conceives, by God's grace, and gives birth to Reuven (see, a son). Her inward chaotic humiliation began to be destroyed by God due to His grace and favor. She now knows her husband will love her. She again cries out to God and has another son, Shim'on (hearing). Again her fear of God has caused His blessing upon her and she gives birth to a third son, Levi (joining).

Le'ah conceives again and has a fourth son, Y'hudah (praise). This unloved wife has built her self-respect by fearing God and seeking Him. In turn God blessed Le'ah and destroyed her chaos and gave her something to praise about. She went from unloved to well-loved and respected by Ya'akov, her husband.

She relied on God to bring her the praise she desperately needed. Feeling worth for herself was of great value. She did not have physical beauty to rely on and her relationship to her sister was very strained. Le'ah looked to the Lord to bring her favor and a much better standing with her husband. What a beautiful and inspirational story of a woman who feared God by acknowledging Him as her sustenance and a way of gaining praise from her family. This story is a great testimony to the letter "Shin". Le'ah was a true women of God who gave birth to the greatest tribe of Israel, Y'hudah (Judah). Her godly works of prayer eventually gave her a place among leaders of the Bible. Jewish women today look to her as an example of building a family.

As life moves forward with the Lord, it is the godliness and fear of God that will cause people to praise a woman at the city gates. The community will discover a family who loves and respects such a wife and a mother. Charm and beauty are going to overridden by a woman who fears the Lord Almighty.

> *"Don't be afraid of what you are about to suffer. Look, the Adversary is going to have some of you thrown in prison, in order to put you to the test; and you will face an ordeal for ten days. Remain faithful,*

even to the point of death; and I will give you life as your crown." (Revelation 2:10).

Let Us Reason Together

What drew you to your spouse? What first got your attention?

Describe your spouse from the outside in!

What is the connection between a beautiful woman and the efforts of advertising?

Develop an action plan to prioritize your pursuits in life. Where will you start?

Are you consumed with envy by woman who rely on their charm and beauty?

What questions, thoughts, or feelings do you have after reading chapter twenty one?

NOTES

NOTES

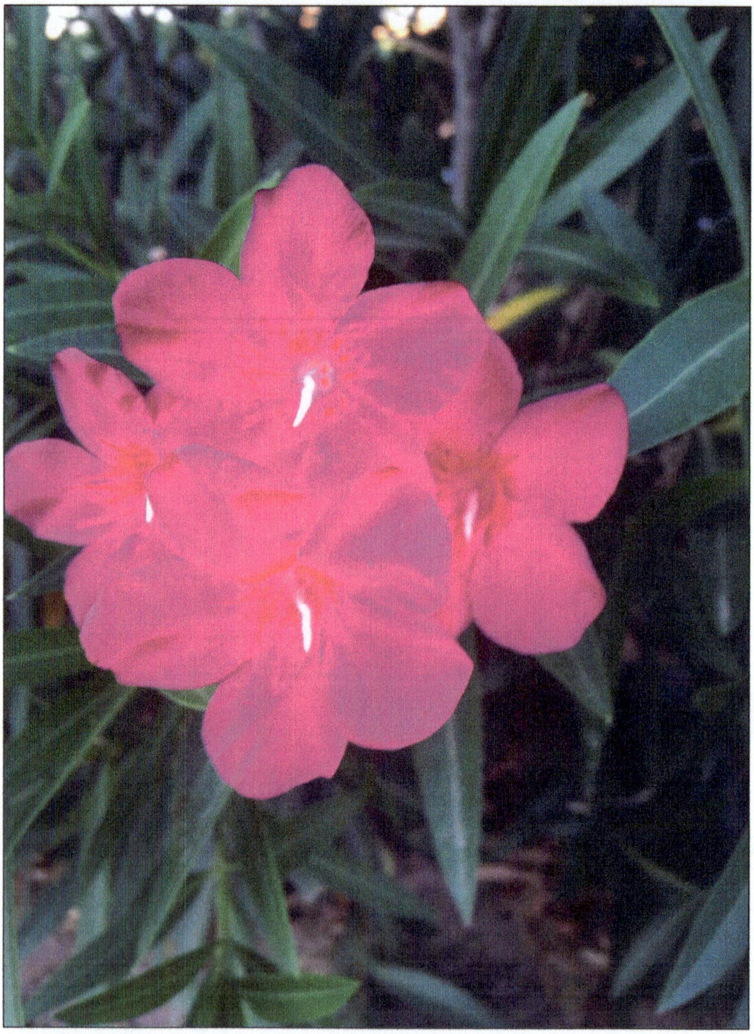

Chapter 22

GIVE HER A SHARE

"Give her a share in what she produces; let her works speak her praises at the city gates." (Proverbs 31:31)

The twenty-second and last letter from the inspired Hebrew alphabet is "Tav" which has the sound of "t" as in "teach."[173] The pictograph shape means a "cross,"[174] "mark, or sign."[175] The symbolic meaning is "covenant"[176] or "seal."[177] Yeshua said He is the "Aleph" and "Tav" (***Revelation 22:13***) which means He is the strength of the cross which is a sign of covenant between God and mankind.

"I am the 'A' and the 'Z', the First and the Last, the Beginning and the End" (Revelation 22:13).

In Ezekiel, God puts this mark "Tav" on the foreheads of His faithful to declare His selection and ownership (***Ezekiel 9***). These covenant people were to be avoided by the executioner who went through the city and killed the rebels against God. Those who worshiped the Lord Almighty and cried out to Him were secured in His well-being and safety by a sign and covenant.

This is the most familiar sign to believers of Yeshua Messiah. It is on the crossbeam mounted to a stake that our Savior willingly gave His life as a bloody sacrificial death. He died on a cross to give believers in Him, an eternal covenant of salvation. We have the sign written upon our hearts and it will secure the shared glory in Him by covenant.

A Hebrew word using the letter "Tav" is "tag" which means crowns or the crownlet on Hebrew letters called "serif."[178] Yeshua said not one "tag" would pass away from His Word, "The Covenant". Another word is "to-rah" which means to "shoot an arrow or hit the mark."[179] This is the teachings and instructions of God to mankind; Genesis, Exodus, Leviticus, Numbers, and Deuteronomy. In some contexts it could also mean the Prophets and Writing. God's Holy Writ is also called the "ta-nakh" which is the Law, Prophets and Writings.[180] The Torah which can be inclusive of the whole of Scripture is God's covenant and a sign to lead the way to external life. His works of salvation through Yeshua, His only begotten Son, by the power of the Spirit, will ring praises at the eternal gates of New Jerusalem.

<u>It is her committed heart in God's eternal covenant that has secured her fair share of what she has produced, spiritually and financially.</u>

This proverb concludes the most wonderful passage of God writings concerning a noble righteous woman. A lesson to listen, learn and live by more richly.[181] She has produced an environment of an anointed righteous home through her faith in Yehovah, while serving Him worshipfully each day. Her love toward her husband and children in practical ways, has given her a place of honor among the home, neighborhood and surrounding community. Her husband has honored her covenantal relationship to him by giving her a share of the inheritance. Actions speak louder than words. It is her committed heart in God's eternal covenant that has secured her fair share of what she has produced, spiritually and financially.

This is a prophetic command to give this noble female a share of her efforts whether financially or in recognition by the people of Israel at the city gates. Giving her a share demonstrates she is living under the covenant of God that was established through Abraham, Isaac, and Jacob. God gave the land of Israel to the Jewish people. Her share or participation in the spiritual and physical riches of the covenantal relationship are a reflection of her hard work.

> *"When the evening came, the owner of the vineyard said to his forearm, 'Call the workers and pay them their wages, starting with the last ones hired and ending with the first" (Matthew 20:8).*

This proverb is a simile of the Kingdom of Heaven. It's more about the generosity of God than about what mankind deems as fair. Just because a wife is a female does not mean she should have less rights to the income she has produced. She has God-given privileges to share in the wealth of the home. Let her have some spending and retirement income herself, as she deems fair. Beside the husband, she is a joint heir in marital covenantal relationship. *"Be strong, be bold" (Joshua 1:6) and take your inheritance.*

As a female who is a descendant of Abraham, there is a covenantal relationship to her and God. She has the blessing to inherit the benefits of her hard labor. A decent husband should give her a fair share of her production due to her taking advantage of wise investment opportunities. Her works are to be a great role model for the younger women at the city gates. These blessings are to be enjoyed and the husband is so blessed to have her as a wife that he takes joy and delight in ensuring she receives a fair share of her efforts.

<u>These blessings are to be enjoyed and the husband is so blessed to have her as a wife that he takes joy and delight in ensuring she receives a fair share of her efforts.</u>

Our Father in heaven gives us a share of the Spirits gifting (*I Corinthians 12*). It does not matter whether we are Jews or Gentiles, slaves or free, male or female. We, by His grace, are marked with the sign of the covenant and will receive the inheritance of the Holy Spirit. Praise Adonai!

> *"If God is concerned about cattle, all the more does he says this for our sakes. Yes, it was written for us,*

meaning that he who plows and he who threshes should work expecting to get a share of the crop" (*1 Corinthians 9:9b-10*).

Those who work to produce should also share in its abundance. Whether it be spiritual, social or material. The divine commission to work also has a divine commission to be honored materially and publically among the family of God. On the human level of life, her works that have served her family well, and even service to humanity as a whole, should laud her at the city gates. This brings glory to the Lord as we read in *Isaiah 29:23a*,

"When his descendants see the work of my hands among them, they will consecrate my name."

As Israel see's the work of God's hands upon them they consecrate His name. This is a role model to follow concerning a righteous woman. She is a visible sign as a reminder of God's covenant and love. They are to honor a virtuous noble wife at the city gates due to her obedience to the Lord. Let her know her efforts are not in vain.

"So, my dear brothers, stand firm and immovable, always doing the Lord's work as vigorously as you can, knowing that united with the Lord your efforts are not in vain" (*1 Corinthians 15:58*).

It is easy to speak highly for such a female. Not only is she fitting for this prophecy in ***Proverbs 31***, she is also is a ***Psalms 15*** saint. Her trustworthy human quality should be proclaimed among the younger women and pre-teen girls. ***Philippians 4:8*** is to be used as we give praise to God for such a wife and woman of God. Let this daughter of Israel, who is under God's covenant, be blessed with such praise.

> *"The king liked Ester more than any of his wives; none of the other virgins obtained such favor and approval from him. So he put the royal crown on her head and made her a queen in place of Vashti."*
> *Ester 2:17*

Let Us Reason Together

What are your strengths as a **Proverbs 31** woman? Your weaknesses?

How does your faith provide encouragement and righteousness living in your home?

In what ways do you enjoy the produce or products of your labor?

If you were to obtain what you think you deserve (regarding your contributions), what would you receive?

Describe your definition of inheritance. What does God's word say about the honor due a faithful **Proverbs 31** woman?

Is your picture next to that definition?

Husbands, what do you need to do to honor your wife?

What questions, thoughts, or feelings do you have after reading chapter twenty two?

NOTES

NOTES

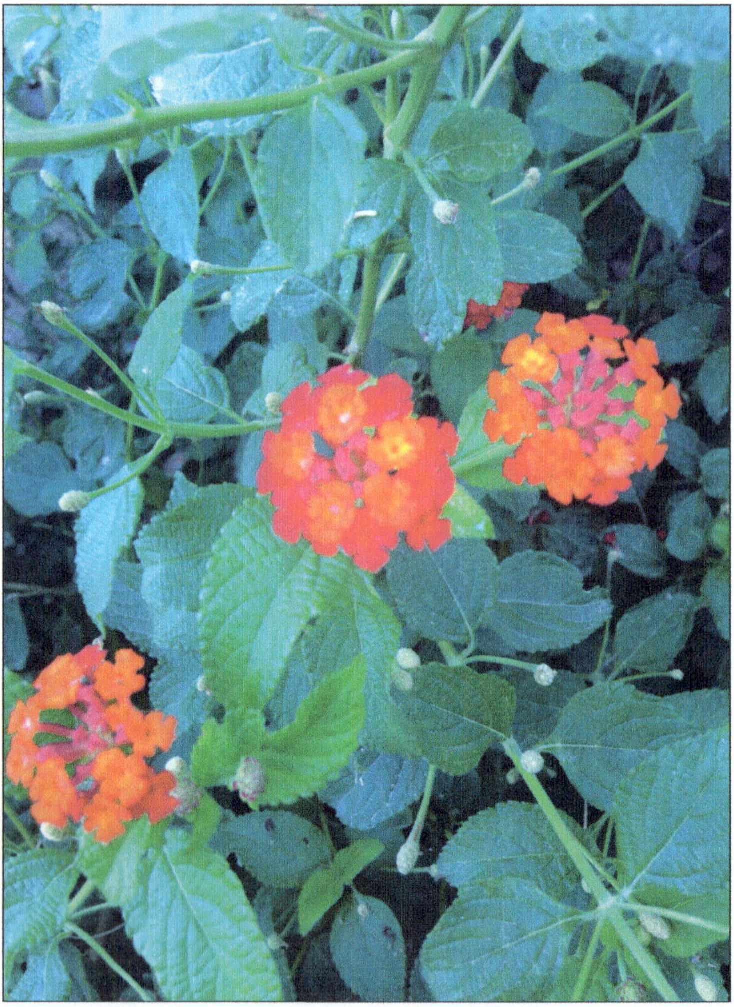

IN CONCLUSION

You have probably experienced an approach to God's Word unlike anything you have ever read or studied before. I surely hope it was a blessing to learn about yourself, as a female, letter by letter with the Hebrew alphabet. To discover that Yeshua Messiah has revealed Himself in and through the complexity and design of a female is unique and very special.

Maybe you have discovered strengths and weaknesses in your spiritual character. Culture and philosophy can damage the real intent and purpose of God's will and expectations but I hope this teaching is a help and simply another piece of the puzzle. I wanted this book to be a tribute and a way to express my heartfelt gratitude for all young and "seasoned" women.

May the Lord heal and restore your heart if you have been abused and wounded. I know the Lord can lead you into a life of forgiveness. I know this teaching has given me a better understanding and respect for women in my family and the community of believers. I have been so inspired to write out this teaching. I know in my heart the Holy Spirit moved me in such a way. He encouraged me by working through other saints to push me to keep diligent in this work, and give honor to all the women who have been a part of my life in Yeshua Messiah.

I believe my Redeemer lives and ever makes intercession for me before my Father in heaven. Yeshua is worthy of all praise and honor. I know women are beautiful and can achieve God's highest expectations as they lean on Him for His ability to work in and through them. Truthfully, I cannot understand the complexity of a female. Her thoughts and emotions at times are difficult to understand. But I have learned and do know this about women. Their lives have proved to me crowns can and do blossom.

> *"For just as rain and snow fall from the sky and do not return there, but water the earth, causing it to bud and produce, giving seed to the sower and bread to the eater; so is my word that goes out from my mouth-it will not return to me unfulfilled; but it will accomplish what I intend, and cause to succeed what I sent it to do." (Isaiah 55:10-11)*

ENDNOTES

Introduction.
[1] The JPS Torah Commentary, Genesis, Nahum M. Sarna, The Jewish Publication Society, Philadelphia, 1989, p.22.
[2] The JPS Torah Commentary, p.21.
[3] The JPS Torah Commentary, p.22.
[4] The JPS Torah Commentary, p.22-23.
[5] The Book of Proverbs a Commentary, W. Gunther Plaut, J.D.S., Union of American Hebrew Congregations, New York, N.Y., 1961, p.316.
[6] The Gospel in Ancient Hebrew, Dr. Frank T. Seekins, Living Word Pictures Inc, Phoenix, Arizona, 2002, p.1.
[7] The Gospel in Ancient Hebrew, p.20.
[8] Jewish Faith and the New Covenant, Ruth Spector Lascelle, Rock of Israel, Van Nuys, CA, 1993, p.570-571.
[9] The Matthew Henry Commentary, New One Volume Edition, Commentary on the Whole Bible by Matthew Henry, edited by Rev Leslie Church Ph.D, F.R.Hist.S.,, Zondervan Publishing House, Grand Rapids, Michigan, 1982, p.787.
[10] Matthew Henry Commentary, p.787.

Chapter 1
[11] Zola's Introduction to Hebrew, John Parsons, Zola Levitt Ministries Inc, Dallas, Texas, 2006, p.9.
[12] The Gospel in Ancient Hebrew, p.20.
[13] The Gospel in Ancient Hebrew, p.20.

[14] Jewish faith and the New Covenant, p.575.
[15] Zola's Introduction to Hebrew, p.339.
[16] Zola's Introduction to Hebrew, p.339.
[17] Zola's Introduction to Hebrew, p.342.

Chapter 2
[18] Zola's Introduction to Hebrew, p.10.
[19] The Gospel in Ancient Hebrew, p.20.
[20] The Gospel in Ancient Hebrew, p.20.
[21] Jewish Faith and the New Covenant, p.576.
[22] Zola's Introduction to Hebrew, p.345.

Chapter 3
[23] Zola's Introduction to Hebrew, p.11.
[24] The Gospel in Ancient Hebrew, p.20.
[25] The Gospel in Ancient Hebrew, p.20.
[26] Jewish Faith and the New Covenant, p.576.
[27] Theological Dictionary of the New Testament, Geoffrey W. Bromiley, William B. Eerdmans Publishing Company, Grand Rapids, Michigan, 1985, p.495.

Chapter 4
[28] Zola's Introduction to Hebrew, p.12.
[29] Zola's Introduction to Hebrew, p.12.
[30] The Gospel in Ancient Hebrew, p.20.
[31] Zola's Introduction to Hebrew, p.352.
[32] The Gospel in Ancient Hebrew, p20.
[33] Zola's Introduction to Hebrew, p.351-352.

Chapter 5
[34] Zola's Introduction to Hebrew, p.13.
[35] Zola's Introduction to Hebrew, p.13.
[36] The Gospel in Ancient Hebrew, p.20.
[37] Jewish Faith and the New Covenant, p.576.
[38] The Gospel in Ancient Hebrew, p.20.
[39] Zola's Introduction to Hebrew, p.353.
[40] Jewish Faith and the New Covenant, p.576.

Endnotes

[41] Zola's Introduction to Hebrew, p.353-354.

Chapter 6
[42] Zola's Introduction to Hebrew, p.23.
[43] Zola's Introduction to Hebrew, p.355.
[44] The Gospel in Ancient Hebrew, p.20.
[45] Jewish Faith and the New Covenant, p.576.
[46] Zola's Introduction to Hebrew, p.355.
[47] Zola's Introduction to Hebrew, p.355.

Chapter 7
[48] Zola's Introduction to Hebrew, p.24.
[49] Zola's Introduction to Hebrew, p.24.
[50] The Gospel in Ancient Hebrew, p.20.
[51] Zola's Introduction to Hebrew, p.356.
[52] The Gospel in Ancient Hebrew, p.20.
[53] Zola's Introduction to Hebrew, p.356.
[54] Zola's Introduction to Hebrew, p.356.

Chapter 8
[55] Zola's Introduction to Hebrew, p.25.
[56] Zola's Introduction to Hebrew, p.358.
[57] The Gospel in Ancient Hebrew, p.20.
[58] The Gospel in Ancient Hebrew, p.20.
[59] The Gospel in Ancient Hebrew, p.20.
[60] Jewish Faith and the New Covenant, p.577.
[61] Zola's Introduction to Hebrew, p.357-358.

Chapter 9
[62] Zola's Introduction to Hebrew, p.26.
[63] The Gospel in Ancient Hebrew, p.20.
[64] Zola's Introduction to Hebrew, p.361.
[65] The Gospel in Ancient Hebrew, p.20.
[66] Zola's Introduction to Hebrew, p.361.

Chapter 10
[67] Zola's Introduction to Hebrew, p.27.

[68] The Gospel in Ancient Hebrew, p20.
[69] Zola's Introduction to Hebrew, p.362.
[70] The Gospel in Ancient Hebrew, p.20.
[71] Jewish Faith and the New Covenant, p.577.
[72] Zola's Introduction to Hebrew, p.362.
[73] Zola's Introduction to Hebrew, p.362.

Chapter 11
[74] Zola's Introduction to Hebrew, p.37.
[75] The Gospel in Ancient Hebrew, p.20.
[76] Jewish Faith and the New Covenant, p.577.
[77] The Gospel in Ancient Hebrew, p.20.
[78] Jewish Faith and the New Covenant, p.577.
[79] Zola's Introduction to Hebrew, p.365.
[80] Zola's Introduction to Hebrew, p.367.
[81] The Book of Proverbs a Commentary, p.314.
[82] Matthew Henry Commentary, p.789.

Chapter 12
[83] Zola's Introduction to Hebrew, p.38.
[84] The Gospel in Ancient Hebrew, p.20.
[85] Jewish Faith and the New Covenant, p.577.
[86] The Gospel in Ancient Hebrew, p.20.
[87] Zola's Introduction to Hebrew, p.369.
[88] Zola's Introduction to Hebrew, p.368.
[89] Zola's Introduction to Hebrew, p.368.
[90] The Book of Proverbs a Commentary, p.314.
[91] The Book of Proverbs a Commentary, p.117.
[92] Jewish Commentary on Proverbs, p.117.

Chapter 13
[93] Zola's Introduction to Hebrew, p.39.
[94] The Gospel in Ancient Hebrew, p.20.
[95] Jewish Faith and the New Covenant, p.577.
[96] The Gospel in Ancient Hebrew, p.20.
[97] Zola's Introduction to Hebrew, p.370.
[98] Zola's Introduction to Hebrew, p.370.

[99] Zola's Introduction to Hebrew, p.371.

Chapter 14
[100] Zola's Introduction to Hebrew, p.40.
[101] Zola's Introduction to Hebrew, p.40.
[102] The Gospel in Ancient Hebrew, p.20.
[103] Zola's Introduction to Hebrew, p.377.
[104] The Gospel in Ancient Hebrew, p.20.
[105] Zola's Introduction to Hebrew, p.378.
[106] Zola's Introduction to Hebrew, p.377.

Chapter 15
[107] Zola's Introduction to Hebrew, p.41.
[108] Zola's Introduction to Hebrew, p.381.
[109] The Gospel in Ancient Hebrew, p.20.
[110] The Gospel in Ancient Hebrew, p.20.
[111] The Gospel in Ancient Hebrew, p.20.
[112] Jewish Faith and the New Covenant, p.577.
[113] Zola's Introduction to Hebrew, p.380.
[114] Zola's Introduction to Hebrew, p.381.
[115] Zola's Introduction to Hebrew, p.381.
[116] Expositors Bible Commentary, p1132.

Chapter 16
[117] Zola's Introduction to Hebrew, p.53.
[118] Zola's Introduction to Hebrew, p.53.
[119] The Gospel in Ancient Hebrew, p.20.
[120] Jewish Faith and the New Covenant, p.577.
[121] The Gospel in Ancient Hebrew, p.20.
[122] Jewish Faith and the New Covenant, p.577.
[123] Zola's Introduction to Hebrew, p.382.
[124] Zola's Introduction to Hebrew, p.383.
[125] Zola's Introduction to Hebrew, p.383.
[126] Zola's Introduction to Hebrew, p.383.

Chapter 17
[127] Zola's Introduction to Hebrew, p.54.

[128] Zola's Introduction to Hebrew, p.54.
[129] The Gospel in Ancient Hebrew, p.20.
[130] The Gospel in Ancient Hebrew, p.20.
[131] Zola's Introduction to Hebrew, p.386.
[132] Jewish Faith and the New Covenant, p.578.
[133] Zola's Introduction to Hebrew, p.386.
[134] Zola's Introduction to Hebrew, p.386.
[135] Zola's Introduction to Hebrew, p.386.
[136] Matthew Henry Commentary, p.789.
[137] Matthew Henry Commentary, p.789.
[138] Expositors Bible Commentary, p.1133.

Chapter 18
[139] Zola's Introduction to Hebrew, p.55.
[140] Zola's Introduction to Hebrew, p.55.
[141] The Gospel in Ancient Hebrew, p20.
[142] Jewish Faith and the New Covenant, p.578.
[143] The Gospel in Ancient Hebrew, p.20.
[144] Zola's Introduction to Hebrew, p.388.
[145] Zola's Introduction to Hebrew, p.388.
[146] Zola's Introduction to Hebrew, p.389.
[147] Expositors Bible Commentary, p.1133.

Chapter 19
[148] Zola's Introduction to Hebrew, p.56.
[149] The Gospel in Ancient Hebrew, p.20.
[150] Zola's Introduction to Hebrew, p.391.
[151] The Gospel in Ancient Hebrew, p.20.
[152] Zola's Introduction to Hebrew, p.390.
[153] Zola's Introduction to Hebrew, p.390.
[154] Expositors Bible Commentary, p.1133.

Chapter 20
[155] Zola's Introduction to Hebrew, p.57.
[156] The Gospel in Ancient Hebrew, p.20.
[157] The Gospel in Ancient Hebrew, p.20.
[158] Zola's Introduction to Hebrew, p.392.

[159] Zola's Introduction to Hebrew, p.393.
[160] Zola's Introduction to Hebrew, p.393.
[161] Zola's Introduction to Hebrew, p.393.

Chapter 21
[162] Zola's Introduction to Hebrew, p.71.
[163] The Gospel in Ancient Hebrew, p.20.
[164] Zola's Introduction to Hebrew, p.398.
[165] The Gospel in Ancient Hebrew, p.20.
[166] Jewish Faith and the New Covenant, p.578.
[167] Zola's Introduction to Hebrew, p.395.
[168] Zola's Introduction to Hebrew, p.396.
[169] Zola's Introduction to Hebrew, p.397.
[170] Zola's Introduction to Hebrew, p.398.
[171] The Book of Proverbs a Commentary, p.315.
[172] The Book of Proverbs a Commentary, p.315.

Chapter 22
[173] Zola's Introduction to Hebrew, p.72.
[174] The Gospel in Ancient Hebrew, p.20.
[175] Zola's Introduction to Hebrew, p.402.
[176] Zola's Introduction to Hebrew, p.402.
[177] The Gospel in Ancient Hebrew, p.20.
[178] Zola's Introduction to Hebrew, p.402.
[179] Zola's Introduction to Hebrew, p.403.
[180] Zola's Introduction to Hebrew, p.404.
[181] The Book of Proverbs a Commentary, p.316.

BIBLIOGRAPHY

The Book of Jewish Knowledge, Nathan Ausubel, Crown Publishers, Inc, New York, USA, 1964.

The Book of Proverbs a Commentary, W. Gunther Plaut, J.S.D., Union of American Hebrew Congregations, New York, N.Y., 1961.

The Expositor's Bible Commentary, Frank E. Gaebelein, The New International Version, Volume 5, Zondervan Publishing House, Grand Rapids, Michigan, 1991.

The Gospel in Ancient Hebrew, Dr. Frank T. Seekins, Living Word Pictures Inc, Phoenix Arizona, 2002.

Jewish Faith and the New Covenant, Ruth Specter Lascelle, Rock of Israel, Van Nuys, CA, 1993.

The JPS Torah Commentary, Genesis, Nahum M. Sarna, The Jewish Publication Society, Phildelphia, 1989.

The Matthew Henry Commentary, New One Volume Edition. Commentary on the Whole Bible by Matthew Henry, edited by Rev Leslie F. Church Ph.D, F.R.Hist.S., Zondervan Publishing House, Grand Rapids, Michigan, 1982.

Sharing the Word, Dr. Frank T. Seekins, Living Word Pictures, Phoenix, Arizona, 2003.

The Ten Commandments: Looking at the Commandments through the Ancient Word Pictures, Dr. Frank T. Seekins, Phoenix, Arizona, 2002.

Theological Dictionary of the New Testament, Geoffrey W. Bromiley, William B. Eerdmans Publishing Company, Grand Rapids, Michigan, 1985.

Vine's Expository Dictionary of Old and New Testament Words, W.E. Vine Old Testament Edited by F.F. Bruce, World Bible Publishers, Iowa Falls, Iowa, 1981.

Zola's Introduction To Hebrew, John Parsons, Zola Levitt Ministries Inc, Dallas, Texas, 2006.

ABOUT THE AUTHOR

Born and raised in El Paso, Texas. Married to Kimberly Dale Brooks. Have two children, Brandon Paul Brooks and Lynne Michelle Brooks Palacio. Seven grandchildren. Worked in the aviation industry as a licensed airframe and powerplant mechanic. Worked on T-38A/B and F4 Phantom jet aircraft under the United States Airforce contracts. Worked as a primary contractor with the NASA Shuttle training program. Currently working with the Homeland Security Customs Border Patrol on helicopters. Attended Southwestern Assembly of God University from 1995-1999 and graduated with a Bachelor of Science in Pastoral Ministries. Served the Lord as a pastoral youth leader and congregational elder. Have had the blessed opportunity to travel to Israel four times and am currently beginning a study in the Hebrew language.

CPSIA information can be obtained at www.ICGtesting.com
Printed in the USA
BVOW10s1713110715

408018BV00048B/329/P